TAKING
THOUGHTS
CAPTIVE

TAKING THOUGHTS CAPTIVE

THE WAR BETWEEN TRUTH AND LIES

RICK THOMAS

TAKING THOUGHTS CAPTIVE:
The War Between Truth and Lies

ISBN 978-1-966741-17-6

Rick Thomas

Edited by Sheron Wallace

Life Over Coffee
8595 Pelham Rd Ste 400 #406,
Greenville, SC 29615
LifeOverCoffee.com

Dedication

To Lucia

One of the purest-thinking people I have ever met.
You take your thoughts captive, subjecting them to the
obedience of Christ. I follow you as you follow Him.

For additional resources, visit

lifeovercoffee.com

Table of Contents

Introduction

Your mind is a battlefield. Every day, you engage in a war of thoughts—truth versus deception, faith versus doubt, God's wisdom versus your wisdom, obedience versus disobedience. What you think determines how you live. The ideas that govern your mind shape your desires, your emotions, and, ultimately, your actions. The Bible speaks directly to this reality:

> We destroy arguments and every lofty opinion raised against the knowledge of God, and take every thought captive to obey Christ.
>
> (2 Corinthians 10:5)

God calls us to take our thoughts captive, to bring them into submission under the authority of Christ. But for many, this is easier said than done. The thoughts that control us often go unchallenged—whether they stem from past experiences, cultural conditioning, or personal desires. This book is a roadmap to winning that war.

Why This Book?

Many Christians live in a double-minded state, torn between what they know to be true and what they desire. They have biblical knowledge but struggle to apply it. They trust God with their salvation but doubt His goodness in their sanctification, especially in their suffering. They believe in His promises but wrestle with fear, anxiety, and disappointment. If you are tired of feeling stuck—tossed about by competing thoughts, overwhelmed by emotions, and discouraged by a lack of lasting change—this book will help. The goal is not merely to modify behavior but to transform thinking at its core. In *Taking Thoughts Captive,* you will:

- Identify the battle between biblical and unbiblical thinking.
- Expose the lies you have unknowingly believed.
- Learn practical strategies to reshape your thought life.
- Apply biblical wisdom to everyday struggles.
- Experience the peace and stability that come from a mind aligned with Christ.

The Journey Ahead

This book is structured as a progression from diagnosing the problem to implementing real change. Each chapter builds upon the last, equipping you with the tools to renew your mind and walk in gospel-centered freedom.

1. **CHAPTER 1—** *The Problem With Head Knowledge Versus Heart Knowledge:* Many Christians fall into the trap of believing that head knowledge (knowing biblical truth) and heart knowledge (acting on it) are separate things. But this cliché is a false distinction that keeps people stuck in disobedience. In reality, both are matters of thought. If your desires contradict biblical understanding, the issue is not an emotional one but a battle of competing thoughts. This chapter lays a strong foundation by helping you understand how double-mindedness keeps you unstable.

2. **CHAPTER 2—** *An Analysis of the Evolution and Superiority of the Christian Mind:* Once we establish that thinking rightly is at the core of Christian living, we must ask: What makes the Christian mind distinct? This chapter explores how the believer's thought life differs from the unbeliever's, revealing why worldly, cultural thinking is insufficient and why biblical wisdom leads to life and godliness.

3. **CHAPTER 3—** *Emotional Problems Point to a Poor Thought Life:* Many assume that emotions and thoughts are separate—that their emotions control them rather than their thinking. But Scripture teaches that our emotions flow from our thoughts. Anxiety, anger, and despair are not random; they are the product of what we dwell on. This chapter will challenge the modern emphasis on "emotional problems" and show how addressing your thought life leads to emotional stability.

4. **CHAPTER 4—** *Learning How to Take Thoughts Captive:* Recognizing that thoughts shape our emotions and actions is one thing; learning how to control those thoughts is another. Paul commands us to take every thought captive to obey Christ. But how? This chapter presents a biblical strategy for recognizing and dismantling unbiblical thinking patterns.

5. **CHAPTER 5—** *Mind Mapping Stinking Thinking: How to Change Your Mind:* If wrong thinking leads to destructive emotions and behaviors, how do we replace those thoughts with biblical ones? This chapter introduces the concept of mind mapping—a practical way to trace wrong beliefs back to their roots and replace them with God's truth.

6. **CHAPTER 6—** *Three Mind Maps on How to Change Your Thought Life:* Building on the previous chapter,

you'll find three specific mind maps that guide you through the process of renewing your thoughts. These practical frameworks will help you take common abstract biblical principles and apply them to real-life struggles.

7. **CHAPTER 7—** *Memories: Forgetting Past Relationship Thoughts:* Our past often holds us hostage. Whether it's regret, bitterness, or longing for a better time, dwelling on past relationships can distort present experiences. This chapter helps you apply biblical thinking to your history, freeing you from the emotional and mental burdens of past relationships.

8. **CHAPTER 8—** *Eight Practical and Transforming Ways to Think About Your Past:* Beyond relationships, many struggle with guilt, shame, or frustration over past failures. This chapter provides eight biblical strategies for reframing your past so that it no longer dictates your future.

9. **CHAPTER 9—** *The Blessing of Doing Things Without Thinking:* Not all habits are bad. In fact, God designed us to function in ways that don't require constant conscious effort. The key is forming good habits that align with biblical thinking. This chapter explores how to develop Christlike instincts and reflexive obedience.

10. **CONCLUSION—** *When Obedience Collides With My Emotions:* We conclude by addressing a crucial reality: There will be times when your thought-driven emotions pull you away from obedience. In those moments, what will you do? This chapter challenges you to obey God even when you don't feel like it, showing how the right actions can shape the right emotions.

A Call to War

This book is not merely an intellectual exercise. It is a battle plan. The enemy wants to keep you double-minded, tossed by waves of fear, doubt, and selfish ambition. But God calls you to be steadfast, transformed by the renewing of your mind (Romans 12:2). If you engage practically with these truths, apply these principles, and take your thoughts captive to Christ, you will not remain the same. A renewed mind leads to a renewed life. Are you ready to take every thought captive? The war is real, but so is the victory. Let's begin.

1

Heart and Head

Some phrases are so catchy that they become part of our Christian vocabulary almost without question. Over time, these sayings turn into clichés—short, memorable expressions that capture an idea. There is nothing inherently wrong with this form of expression. A well-crafted phrase can serve as a helpful reminder of biblical truths. But when a cliché lacks theological depth and precision, it can do more harm than good. One such phrase is the distinction between head knowledge and heart knowledge.

The concept suggests that knowing the right theological thing intellectually (head knowledge) is not enough—what truly matters is whether that truth has reached the heart (heart knowledge). The false assumption is that the heart operates independently from the mind, creating a line of division between what we believe in our heads and what we embrace in our hearts. While this sounds compelling on its face, it is an unhelpful and misleading way to think about how we process truth.

The problem with this phrase is that it implies two kinds of knowledge, as though biblical truth must take an added step to move from the head to the heart. But in reality, what we call head knowledge and heart knowledge are both matters of the same thing—our thoughts. They are not two separate categories of understanding something but rather different kinds of thinking—one aligned with God's wisdom and the other entangled in unbiblical desires.

What Is It?

When someone says, "I have head knowledge, but I need heart knowledge," they often mean that they understand what the Bible says but struggle to live according to that truth. They are describing a conflict between what they know is right and what they desire—idolize—in their hearts. Consider a Christian who knows that worrying is a sin but still feels overwhelmed with anxiety. They might say, "I know in my head that God is sovereign, but my heart is still fearful." But is their heart the issue? No, their thinking is the issue. They are caught between believing that God is in control and entertaining fearful thoughts that contradict that belief. The real problem is not an emotional one but a battle between two competing thought patterns—one biblical, one unbiblical.

Another example is Mable, who is angry with her husband, Biff. She knows that her anger is sinful and that God calls her to respond with patience and grace. She says, "I have head knowledge, but my heart is not quite there yet." Again, this is not a heart problem—but a thinking problem. She knows what is right but is allowing unbiblical thoughts (idols) about Biff's shortcomings to govern her emotions, which drive her ungodly actions toward him.

The Connection

Some Christians might push back and say, "But heart knowledge is about emotions, not just thoughts." This argument is where we must recognize the direct link between the two. Emotions are not separate from thoughts—they flow from them. What we think about determines how we respond practically and emotionally.

Imagine that someone deposits a million dollars into your bank account. How would you respond? You would likely feel joy and excitement, not because of some abstract emotional reaction but because you believe something good has happened. Now imagine that, moments later, someone points a gun at you, threatening to take your money. Your feelings would immediately shift from joy to terror, not because your heart independently decided to be afraid but because your mind registered the danger and triggered an emotional response. The formula is simple:

- Right thinking leads to the right emotions.
- Wrong thinking leads to wrong emotions.

If your emotions are out of control, the solution is not to search for some elusive heart knowledge. The solution is to examine what you are thinking wrongly about and realign those wayward thoughts with Scripture.

Double-Mindedness

James describes this battle in striking terms:

> If any of you lacks wisdom, let him ask God, who gives generously to all without reproach, and it will be given him. But let him ask in faith, with no doubting, for the one who doubts is like a wave of the sea that is driven and tossed by the wind. For that person must not suppose that he will receive anything from the Lord; he is a double-minded man, unstable in all his ways.
>
> (James 1:5-8)

A double-minded person knows the truth, but they still entertain unbiblical thoughts. Like our fictional Mable, they intellectually acknowledge God's wisdom but hold onto desires, fears, or frustrations that contradict it. This posture leads to instability—an ongoing oscillation between trust and doubt, obedience and disobedience, joy and discouragement. As long as Mable lives in that double-minded space, she will never experience the shalom of the soul or the restoration of her marriage.

What is the solution? James makes it clear: we must fully submit our thoughts to God's wisdom. If Mable wants to experience peace, she must stop feeding her anger with unbiblical thoughts about her husband. Instead of fixating on his shortcomings, she must meditate on what is true, honorable, and praiseworthy (Philippians 4:8). Only then will she find stability.

Capturing Thoughts

Paul also speaks to this issue in 2 Corinthians 10:3-5, where he describes the Christian life as spiritual warfare:

> For though we walk in the flesh, we are not waging war according to the flesh. For the weapons of our warfare are not of the flesh but have divine power to destroy strongholds. We destroy arguments and every lofty opinion raised against the knowledge of God, and take every thought captive to obey Christ.

Notice that Paul does not say we should focus on taking our emotions captive. He says we must take our thoughts captive. The battle is fought and won at the level of our thinking. If we allow our minds to be ruled by lies, we will be ruled by emotions that reflect those lies. If we discipline our minds to focus on the truth, our emotions will follow the truth in our minds. This shift is not to say that change is easy. Mable, Biff, and all struggling Christians must actively work to align their thinking with God's Word. This work requires continual prayer, meditation on what is true, and seeking counsel from wise believers. It also requires an intentional rejection of thoughts that do not conform to Christ's truth.

Single-Minded Faith

The idea of head knowledge versus heart knowledge is a well-intentioned but misleading phrase. It falsely suggests that our hearts operate separately from our thoughts when, in reality, they are the same. The true battle is not between our heads and hearts but between biblically wise and unbiblically wise thinking. James calls this battle of the soul double-mindedness. Paul calls it a war between good and evil for our thoughts. Whatever terminology we use, the principle remains: to grow in godliness, we must bring every thought under the authority of Christ. As you work through this book, you will learn more about the nature of the Christian mind, how wrong thinking leads to emotional instability, and how to take practical steps to renew your mind. This problem is not a quick fix. It is a lifelong process of taking every thought captive and replacing falsehood with truth.

> Finally, brothers, whatever is true, whatever is honorable, whatever is just, whatever is pure, whatever is lovely, whatever is commendable, if there is any excellence, if there is anything worthy of praise, think about these things.
>
> (Philippians 4:8)

Call to Action

1. What thoughts dominate your mind?
2. Are you allowing double-mindedness to rule your thinking?
3. Where do you need to repent and realign your thoughts with God's truth?
4. Now that you understand the problem with the head knowledge versus heart knowledge cliché, what will you do about it? Recognizing that your thoughts—not your emotions—are at the core of your struggles is only the first step.

Your next move is intentional action. If you continue allowing unbiblical thoughts to run unchecked, you will remain double-minded, unstable, and easily swayed by desires that conflict with God's truth. But if you take your thoughts captive and submit them to Christ, you will grow in clarity, stability, and obedience. Here are a few steps to help you move from double-mindedness to a biblically renewed mind:

1. **EXAMINE YOUR THOUGHTS DAILY:** Are you thinking biblically about your life, circumstances, and relationships? Ask yourself, "What is the root of my frustration, fear, or discouragement?" Trace those emotions back to the thoughts that fuel them.
2. **IDENTIFY COMPETING DESIRES:** Is there something you want so badly that it is leading you to think and act in unbiblical ways? Like Mable, are you demanding a good thing (e.g., a better marriage, a faithful friend, someone to recognize you at work) in a way that breeds and fuels frustration and anger? Ask God to realign your desires with His will.
3. **TAKE YOUR THOUGHTS CAPTIVE:** When you recognize thoughts that are not in line with God's Word, do not let them sit idly in your mind. Actively

challenge them with Scripture. What verse speaks directly to your situation? Meditate on that verse, memorize it, and employ it to combat false thinking.

4. **REPLACE LIES WITH TRUTH:** It's not enough to remove wrong thoughts; you must replace them with the right ones. As Philippians 4:8 instructs, we must dwell on what is true, honorable, just, pure, lovely, and commendable. Fill your mind with biblical wisdom rather than cultural mantras or self-focused reasoning.

5. **SEEK ACCOUNTABILITY:** Do not battle your thoughts alone. Share your struggles with a trusted friend, pastor, or mentor who can help you see your blind spots and challenge your thinking with biblical truth.

6. **PRAY FOR A SINGLE-MINDED HEART:** Ask God to give you a steadfast mind that is fully aligned with His wisdom. Pray as the psalmist did: "Teach me your way, O Lord, that I may walk in your truth; unite my heart to fear your name" (Psalm 86:11).

7. **COMMIT TO ONGOING RENEWAL:** Changing your thought life is not a one-time event but a lifelong process. As you move forward in this book, continue examining your thoughts, aligning them with Scripture, and seeking to glorify God in your thinking.

The war for your mind is real. If you do nothing, you will remain unstable, caught between what you know to be true and what you want at the moment. But if you actively take intentional and practical steps to renew your thoughts, you will experience the peace and clarity that come from a single-minded devotion to Christ.

So, what will you do today to bring your thinking into submission to God's Word?

2

Evolution of the Mind

Our minds are an integral part of ourselves that establishes a definitive trajectory for how we live well in God's world. Did you know the Christian mind evolves into four different types? Like mile-markers up the interstate, we begin with one type of mind, and then it evolves into better versions, aiming for the purest kind of mind a person can have, which is the mind of Christ. As you consider the four types, what kind of mind do you have? Where are you in this four-step progression? Let's analyze the evolution of the Christian mind.

External Developers

When you think about your mind, what comes to mind? How would you describe your mind? What has shaped you mentally? What controls your headspace? Do you know what influences your thinking? It is not just how God made you, but there are outside influences. People, worldviews, culture, memories, and life circumstances form the content of your mind. That which shapes your mind also manages your mind. Because we are not self-reliant, independent beings, we subject our minds to these external developers. Only the Lord is independent and self-sufficient enough to transcend sublunary shaping influences. He is never under the control of anything other than Himself because there is nothing more powerful than God. We are the dependent ones, which leaves us vulnerable to powerful external influences. The good news is that our imminent vulnerabilities do not leave us without hope because Christ is the great power who destroys strongholds and brings every evil thing under His authority (2 Corinthians 10:3-5; 1 John 4:4).

Thus, we have choices. We can determine what type of subordinate mind we want. There is the mind of Adam, and there is the mind of Christ. Of course, between these two, there is the hybrid mind, which is a unique mixture of Adam and Christ. When the new believer receives the mind of Christ at his new birth, it does not decouple him from his former manner of life, which I'm calling the hybrid mind. He hopes to gradually put off that deceitful, troubling mind and renew it more and more into the mind of Christ.

> To put off your old self, which belongs to your former manner of life and is corrupt through deceitful desires, and to be renewed in the spirit of your minds, and to put on the new self, created after the likeness of God in true righteousness and holiness.
>
> (Ephesians 4:22-24).

The Dark Mind

> They are darkened in their understanding, alienated from the life of God because of the ignorance that is in them, due to their hardness of heart. They have become callous and have given themselves up to sensuality, greedy to practice every kind of impurity.
>
> (Ephesians 4:18-19)

The mind of Adam is totally depraved. There is no nook or cranny of mental real estate that the deceitfulness of sin has not corrupted (Ephesians 4:22). Have you ever been inside a dark room? I'm talking about a completely dark room. No light exists. I have. You cannot see your hand in front of your face. It reminds me of what the Lord told Moses when plaguing Egypt.

> And the LORD said unto Moses, "Stretch out your hand toward heaven, that there may be darkness over the land of Egypt, a darkness to be felt."
>
> (Exodus 10:21)

The dark mind is under a similar plague of painful felt hopelessness and helplessness.

1. There is an alienation from God.
2. The dark soul attempts to press God's truth out of their mind (Romans 1:18; 2 Corinthians 4:4).
3. The Lord is in opposition to them, warring against their proud, mental posturing (James 4:6).
4. If the proud soul does not cease their waywardness, he spirals into unremitting and inexhaustible corruption (cf. Romans 1:18-32).
5. Eventually, the Lord will remove the corrupt from the possibility of redemption by turning the dark mind over to feed on itself (Romans 1:24, 26).
6. The only recourse the dark mind has for survival is to become incrementally desensitized to the agitation and antagonism of God's penetrating light—which is not survival at all, but a hardening effect to escape the pressure of God's wrath weighing down on them (cf. John 3:19, 1 Timothy 4:2, and Hebrews 4:7).
7. The dark mind is in a hopeless battle with itself. It will eventually succumb to compounded

corruptness and ever-increasing darkness until the Lord banishes them to the ultimate outer darkness, where all hope for rescue is lost (Matthew 13:42; Revelation 20:15).

The Spiritual Mind

Have this mind among yourselves, which is yours in Christ Jesus, [who did] nothing from rivalry or conceit, but in humility counted others more significant than Himself. He looked not only to His interests but also to the interests of others.

(from Philippians 2:3-8)

The antithetical alternative to the dark mind is the God-given spiritual one (1 Corinthians 2:14). This mind replaces the mind of Adam with the mind of Christ. The last Adam defeats the first Adam. One of the benefits of this spiritual takeover is a new mind that comes from a regenerative and transformative work that only God can grant (cf. John 3:7; Romans 12:1-2; 2 Corinthians 5:17; Galatians 2:20; Ephesians 4:23-24). The Lord is the new shaping influence (potter) of the jar of clay (Isaiah 64:8; 2 Corinthians 4:7).

The regenerated person subjects their mind to the Lord (1 Corinthians 6:19-20). Father God begins a long and drawn-out process of restorative work in those re-born from above (Ephesians 2:10). This new, efficacious work is progressive sanctification. This incremental process unfolds into a beautiful vessel that reflects the image of Christ (2 Corinthians 3:18). Because God's work in us is progressive and incremental, His Spirit does not entirely rule the new, spiritual mind. The Christian's life is a mixed bag of good and bad fruit.

Now the works of the flesh are evident: sexual immorality, impurity, sensuality, idolatry, sorcery, enmity, strife, jealousy, fits of anger, rivalries, dissensions, divisions, envy, drunkenness, orgies, and things like these. (v. 22) But the fruit of the Spirit is love, joy, peace, patience, kindness, goodness, faithfulness, gentleness, self-control; against such things, there is no law. And those who belong to Christ Jesus have crucified the flesh with its passions and desires. If we live by the Spirit, let us also keep in step with the Spirit.

(Galatians 5:19-21a, 22-25)

The Hybrid Mind

If any of you lacks wisdom, let him ask God, who gives generously to all without reproach, and it will be given him. But let him ask in faith, with no doubting, for the one who doubts is like a wave of the sea that is driven and tossed by the wind. For that person must not suppose that he will receive anything from the Lord; he is a double-minded man, unstable in all his ways.

(James 1:5-8)

The battle between good and evil continues to rage in our minds (Romans 7:21-25; 2 Corinthians 10:3-6). All Christians struggle with Adamic baggage—our former manner of life. When James talked about this dilemma, he called it double-mindedness—a Christian wavering somewhere between light and darkness. One day, you are up; the next day, you are down. Like a leaf in the wind, tossed by its whims, two competing masters control the unstable person (Matthew 6:24).

You might never know what you will get from the hybrid person if you're unsure who controls their minds. The aim is to be steadily morphing into the person of Christ. To morph does not refer to an outward appearance of Christ but to taking on the internal qualities of Christ. Becoming transformed into Christ is not—so much—a behavioral exercise as an inner change of the mind's primary shaping influence.

Every Christian wants to relinquish their control center to the person and work of Jesus Christ as illuminated, enabled, and empowered by the Spirit of God and guided by the Word of God. The farther you go in this process of Christlikeness, the more stable you will become. The desire to reposition and restructure our minds to Christlikeness is counterintuitive to the independent, self-reliant spirit of the Adamic person and the Zeitgeist of this age.

The Mind of Christ

We are moving from our old selves to the mind of Christ, maturing to where we are functioning primarily on the redemptive side of our hybrid state. This grace gift is why we have the Bible. God's Word will change our minds in every good way. The Bible's goal is not primarily to make us better theologians—those who study God—but to help us apply our study of God into practical day-to-day living that spreads His fame while considering others more significant than ourselves (Philippians 2:3-4).

Suppose you have the mind of Christ (salvation), and you're regularly transforming into His mind (sanctification). If so, just like Jesus, you will be the beneficiary of a huge amount of Spirit-illuminated and Spirit-empowered other-centered awareness. Jesus was constantly discerning others to learn how He could best serve them (John 2:24-25). His constant surveillance of His sphere of influence positioned Him to help them mature into Christlikeness (John 11:14-15).

He counted the interests of others more significant than His own. The word interests in Philippians 2:4 carries the idea of "fill in the blank." It means you should know others so well that you can place any interest in that space—an interest that would serve them in becoming more like Christ. You do this as a student of God and others. When your mind becomes so saturated with the interests of God and the interests of others, you will have Christ's mind.

Don't Isolate

We need others to have the mind of Christ. We need them for two reasons: so we can serve them and because we cannot have victory over sin without them—the body of Christ. One of the Adamic deceptions is to value isolation over community. People who struggle the most are the most isolated from others. When Adam sinned, his first action was to distance himself from God and His help. If you want the mind of Christ to be your mental default, you must immerse yourself in the lives of other people, and I'm not talking about your favorite social media outlet. It would be best if you had a practical place to be Jesus to others, and that community would guard you against falling back into those Adamic tendencies.

Lord, work so deeply in my heart that I'm freed from the bondage of self-centeredness and given the disposition to look not only to my own interests but also to the interests of others.

– John Piper

Call to Action

What kind of mind do you have? If you have not been born again, you have the mind of Adam. If you have been born again, you have a combination of Adam's mind and the mind of Christ. To determine how you rank on this hybrid scale, you need to analyze your unselfish versus selfish mind war. Here are a few questions I hope will aid you as you think about your mental progression. Perhaps you would find this exercise more beneficial if you shared it with a friend.

1. Has the Lord regenerated you? If you are not a Christian but would like to become one, please contact us.
2. How is the Bible changing you? Be clear and practical as you think about where you were, where you are, and how the Bible aids you in the journey.
3. What is the number one hindrance that stunts your growth in Christ? Perhaps you have a life-dominating habit that you have yet to submit to God's power.
4. What are you doing to remove this hindrance? One of the primary reasons we don't overcome our habits is that we won't share our problems with others.
5. How aware are your friends of this sin pattern, and how are they serving you to overcome it?
6. What else should you do to enjoy a fuller expression of the mind of Christ? What have I not asked? What do you know to do but have yet to do it (James 4:17)?

3

Emotional Problems

Your emotions can be good or bad, but in either case, they accurately reflect what is happening in your thought life. If the emotions are right, the person is thinking and responding correctly. If a person's emotions are not biblically aligned with God's Word, they need intentional, compassionate, and patient biblical care to help change their thinking. Let me illustrate.

- Mable came to counseling on the verge of an emotional breakdown, so she said.
- Marge asked how she could work through the emotional abuse from her husband.
- Mildred has concerns about her erratic emotional problems.

All three of these ladies have self-diagnosed themselves as struggling with their emotions. They have convinced themselves that they have emotional problems. All three of them are most definitely struggling with something, but none of them have emotional problems in the way they think they do. Their emotions are working fine—just as God designed them to work. Their emotions are working well enough to signal that something is amiss in their lives. This ability to perceive what is happening in and around you is a mercy from the Lord.

The real issue for these ladies is not primarily about their emotions but about their thought life and thinking habits. Emotions cannot be damaged or abused. Unfortunately, our psychologized culture has made many crucial inroads regarding the way many Christians think about emotions. For example, abusing emotions could be analogous to abusing smoke. If I tried to harm smoke, I suppose I could wield a ball bat and take a swing at some smoke. According to secular theorists, I would be a smoke abuser.

Smoke abuse, like emotional abuse, is impossible. If you buy into the term emotional abuse, you'll have to look outside the Bible for help, which will be futile. But, if you want to stop unwanted emotional fluctuations in your life, you will need to discern the real source of those up and down emotions, which is always in a person's thought patterns. This worldview regarding Mable, Marge, and Mildred is life-changing: it addresses their thoughts and stabilizes their emotions.

Proper Emotions Illustrated

Let's pretend you were casually walking across a busy intersection downtown. Then, out of nowhere, a speeding car whizzes by you, going 55 MPH. Your eyes widen, your heart races, and you quickly jump back in horror. From an emotional perspective, you're a mess. What triggered your emotions? It was your racing thoughts that amplified in a nanosecond and went in five different directions at once. As for your emotions? They were working as God intended. Your emotions were responding to how you were thinking at that intersection.

How about this: you just received a phone call saying you won a brand-new digital tablet. Now, you're the celebrating one rather than the terrified tourist in the prior illustration. You shriek and bolt upstairs to let your spouse know the good news. You are ecstatic. Again, your emotions are working well and are consistent with your celebratory thoughts. Perhaps you received another phone call that was not as pleasant. Someone just informed you that a family member passed away in the early morning hours. You end the call and sit sadly on the edge of your bed, reflecting. In all three of these case studies, your emotions are reacting to your thoughts, which is normal because emotions are always normal, and so are yours.

Of course, there are times when your emotions are not helpful and need to change. The process for doing this begins by tracing the emotion back to your thought life. It is in your thoughts where your emotions originate. Here is another illustration: suppose you held a rock about the size of your fist above your head. You release the rock. It falls to the ground. You would not suggest that you had a gravity problem. Gravity does what gravity always does. Gravity is being itself, which is also the nature of emotions: they do what they are supposed to do. It's a psychological law: thinking produces comparable and proportional emotions.

Dangerous Minds

Some thoughts can lead to unpleasant emotions. In such cases, the person must begin to change their thinking to have better emotional responses. A happy person is merry in his heart. A habitually angry person has a bitter heart. We are true to ourselves: what we show on the outside is what we are on the inside (Luke 6:43-45; Proverbs 23:7). If you want to change your emotional outside self, you must first adjust your thinking on the inside. For example, here is a list of bad emotions (or reactions) that point to an unbiblical thought life.

POUTING: The pouting person is using a manipulating emotion to show that he is not getting his way. When you see a person pouting, you should immediately know what he is thinking. Anger and manipulation are working in his thought life. If this is a child, it would be easy to respond to him wrongly by giving him the thing that he is manipulating you to give him. The better response to the pouter is to identify what is going on in his mind. More than likely, his thoughts are not biblical. He has a worship disorder that tempts him to cave to his selfish desires rather than esteem others more significantly than himself (Philippians 2:3). You will need to call him to repentance. If you don't, you could validate this type of behavior, which would motivate him to employ it regularly to satisfy all of his selfish thoughts.

CONVICTION: This kind of emotional manifestation is from a person who is feeling terrible about what he has done. He needs explicit biblical intervention. Several things could be going on in their mind. If it is an unbiblical conviction—he is not guilty of anything—he must remove it because it is not from God. There are many Christians who are weighed down by self-imposed forms of guilty regret for things that have happened in their past, whether it was because of them or because of someone else. It is common for parents to rear their children improperly because of lingering guilt that remains in their lives. They parent their children from a position of fear because they feel they have displeased God in some way.

Maybe they had an unbiblical divorce, or the marriage dissolution was not primarily their fault. Rather than living in the freedom of God's forgiveness, they over-compensate and spoil their child by giving him whatever he wants. This tactic is the parent's way of paying for what they did to the child because of the divorce. You might hear them say, "I've asked God to forgive me many times for what I did." The practicalization of the gospel is not real to them. They can't believe God will forgive them by merely asking. God's grace is sufficient, no matter what they did. But because of their poor theology, they feel a sense of conviction that is a product of their thinking rather than from the Spirit of God.

ANGER: The angry person typically is manipulative. Most of the time, he uses his angry emotions to regain control of his world. If you fall prey to his emotion, you will respond precisely how he wants you to respond—in fear—and give in to his manipulations. But suppose the situation permits you to confront him because you know you are not in harm's way. In that case, you may be able to help him understand the corrupted thinking that motivates him to manipulate others emotionally.

You want to speak into his thought life. I realize that in many of these types of situations, which primarily involve women, this redemptive option is not an option. Typically, the wife needs to contact her pastor or other spiritual authority for help. The angry man is playing god. Rather than placing his trust in the Lord to bring about a specific desire, he chooses to circumvent God's way for his sinful purposes. He can—and might—use any means necessary to justify his position while blaming you for what is wrong. Anger is a form of insanity: it's not in line with a biblical mind. It is also a manifestation of insecurity or what the Bible calls fear of man (Proverbs 29:25).

DESPAIR: This is the emotion of the hopeless. According to the discouraged person's thinking, they have lost all hope, and what you are observing by their sad emotional response are forms of despair, grief, worry, or depression. Typically, the despairing person didn't fall into the ditch of despair without a long trail leading to it. It is usually the accumulative effect of many years of poor thinking that has gone unchecked. It is hard to discern this kind of thinking because a person who allows their thoughts to run along these lines for years is not usually forthcoming about what they have been thinking about due to embarrassment.

You may not be aware of how they have been processing things until full-fledged despair has overtaken them. When helping a person like this, you must remember that you will need to be patient but firm with them (1 Thessalonians 5:14). Don't let their emotional despair override your care. You may be tempted to coddle the discouraged person when what they need is compassionate, faith-filled, and courageous grace.

JEALOUSY: This attitude is another form of anger. The jealous thinker is upset about something they are not receiving. They have a coveting thought life, and what you observe on the emotional outside is a jealous attitude of the mind. This struggler does not need your coddling; they need you to bring them back to the cross of Christ. How can the jealous thinking coveter continue in his coveting while responding to the cross? His thoughts need a crucial recalibrated gospel reorientation.

FEAR: This emotional attitude of the heart is the most common emotion of them all. "Do not fear" is the oft-repeated command or appeal in the Bible. Our entire Adamic makeup stands upon the fear/unbelief dynamic that can run wild in our minds. We are born fearful, and we express our fears emotionally. No person can escape this emotion altogether. While at times it can serve us well, as in the case of the terrified tourist, it can also be our worst enemy. The fear-based person needs the gospel just like all of the other people that I have described in this shortlist of dangerous emotions. And what does fear say about our thinking? It means we are not trusting God.

"Do not fear, trust me."

These five words can transform you. All of God's servants have yielded to fearful temptations, but God is greater than all of our shortcomings. If God is for you, then who can be against you (Romans 8:31)? When you are struggling with doubt and fear, merely utter these simple but potent five words. I realize it will take more work than a mantra, but minimally, it is a good start. Go ahead and say them now: "Do not fear, trust me." You must know that God is entirely trustworthy no matter what you may be going through at any given moment. Repeat this truth often. Let it transform your mind and massage your soul: Do not fear; trust God!

Emotional Checkup

When caring for your friends, don't become confused by what you observe behaviorally. Let what you see be clues that take you deeper into their hearts—to their minds. Start with their emotions and move inward to what they are thinking. Once you get into their thought life, ask God to give you the discernment to truly understand what they are thinking and how their thoughts are affecting them. Solving wrong thinking in one meeting would be rare. Often, this type of work takes several meetings, many people, and different contexts to practically speak into a person's life who has had their thinking shaped in unbiblical ways for years. Paul's exhortation in 1 Thessalonians has been meaningful to me as I think about people who need long-term biblical care:

> And we urge you, brothers, admonish the idle, encourage the fainthearted, help the weak, be patient with them all.
>
> (1 Thessalonians 5:14)

Call to Action

1. When you experience strong emotions, do you take time to trace them back to your thoughts? What patterns do you see in your thinking that may be shaping your emotions?

2. Do you tend to blame your emotions for your struggles, or do you recognize that your thoughts drive your emotions? How does this perspective change the way you respond to uncomfortable feelings?

3. Which of the dangerous emotions listed—pouting, conviction, anger, despair, jealousy, or fear—do you struggle with the most? What specific thought patterns fuel these emotions in your life?

4. How do you respond when someone expresses strong emotions? Do you tend to focus only on their feelings, or do you seek to understand and address the fueling thoughts that are shaping their emotions?

5. In what ways do you need to renew your mind with biblical truth so that your emotions align more with God's Word? What steps will you take this week to meditate on and apply Scripture to your thought life?

4

Taking Thoughts Captive

Have you ever accused yourself of something that was not true? It's when you gaslight yourself, telling yourself something that is false. Any false argument launched against yourself can quickly turn into a mental stronghold that could debilitate you spiritually. We are susceptible to false arguments that can take control of our minds. These recurring thought patterns, when left unchecked, will become the dominating arguments of our minds, even to the point where they become our new truth—our new way of thinking. A stronghold is the instrument that shapes how we interpret and respond to life.

Those Old Thoughts

For though we walk in the flesh, we are not waging war according to the flesh. For the weapons of our warfare are not of the flesh but have divine power to destroy strongholds. We destroy arguments and every lofty opinion raised against the knowledge of God, and take every thought captive to obey Christ, being ready to punish every disobedience, when your obedience is complete.

(2 Corinthians 10:3-6)

Mable was such a person. Fear bound her. Some call it insecurity, which is an appropriate term. She was a young, insecure woman who was preoccupied with the arguments that swirled in her head. The controlling opinion of others was a stronghold that Mable seemingly could not break. Even though she knew God's opinion of her was perfect because of Christ, she was not able to live in the freedom of His empowering favor. Early in life, Mable figured out how performing for others was the way to be accepted. Her daddy taught through his passive parenting style, and in the brief moments when he did say something, it was not encouraging. Her childhood experiences shaped her as a people-pleaser. She was motivated not to disappoint others so she would not incur their displeasure.

She became all things to all people with the hope that they would accept her, and though she was excited during her early years with Christ, the old paths of disapproving arguments eventually came back. Mable was never able to break this stronghold successfully. She never learned how to take every thought captive. She knew how to be saved, but she did not mature in her sanctification the way she had hoped. Her former manner of life, which was corrupt through deceptive desires, tempted her to continue to work for acceptance, approval, love, and respect from others. The dominance of these strongholds led her to despair.

Spiritual Warfare

To put off your old self, which belongs to your former manner of life and is corrupt through deceitful desires, and to be renewed in the spirit of your minds, and to put on the new self, created after the likeness of God in true righteousness and holiness.
(Ephesians 4:22-24)

Losing hope, Mable continued to live the way she always lived. She had not learned how to successfully renew her mind according to true right living and true holiness. She was an unbelieving believer—a Christian continuing to live according to an un-Christian quality of life (Mark 9:24). Mable was in warfare with her mind. She was under attack. According to Paul, this was more than just a human living as a human while being in conflict with humans. Mable also lives in a spiritual world where there are real demonic forces who are out to destroy the knowledge of Christ that is resident in her. The evil spiritual world cannot utterly destroy any Christian because Satan is not God's evil equal. Still, there are active, demonic forces that would enjoy nothing more than to derail a child of God from making His name great.

- Plan A for the devil is to keep all people from believing in Christ.
- Plan B for the devil is to keep all Christians from maturing in Christ.

Believing the Lie

Paul called what I am describing spiritual warfare in 2 Corinthians 10:3-6. He viewed his Christian life in warfare terms. He knew where the primary battle came from, and this knowledge served him well in his unceasing fight for his sanctification.

> For though we walk in the flesh, we are not waging war according to the flesh.
>
> (2 Corinthians 10:3)

- Do you know you are in spiritual warfare?
- Do you know that a constant spiritual battle is taking place in this world and that you are part of it?

- Do you know that you are not a sideline reporter but an active participant?

And the LORD said to Satan, "Behold, all that he has is in your hand. Only against him do not stretch out your hand." So Satan went out from the presence of the Lord.

(Job 1:12)

What Paul is teaching us is not new. Spiritual warfare has been going on since Adam and Eve took their first bite of disobedience. The devil tried to knock them off, succeeding to a degree, and he and his minions seek to circumvent the work of God in your life, too.

- Do you know you have weapons to fight these spiritual battles—weapons that are divinely empowered?
- Do you know God designed these weapons with the power to destroy the strongholds in your mind?

Mable did not know this. One of the tricks of the evil one is to disorient and deceive. Deception is what Satan did to Eve, which is what was happening to Mable. Like her fallen predecessors, she had bought the lie. She had learned to believe there was something wrong with her—and God.

What Is a Stronghold?

Owning her faith and living as a new creation in Christ were encouraging theological ideas that had a limited effect on her. She was so wrapped up in her fear that she did not know how to live in the freedom and power that God's gospel provides. The forces that are against you in the spirit world are no different from the forces that are against you in the physical world in that they both desire the same thing: to take your mind captive. The real question is how are you going to respond and fight against the forces that are against you, regardless of what constitutes these forces. You have the power resident within you to fight against the strongholds that seek to take your mind captive. These weapons of warfare are the divinely empowered truths of the gospel.

The real question is whether you will use these weapons to destroy the strongholds—the arguments and arrogant opinions that are raised against God's revealed truth. A stronghold is a mental argument that stands in opposition to God. We believe it, and it contradicts the person and power of Christ. A stronghold is a thought fortress of arguments designed to take our minds captive and hold us as prisoners. These fortresses are intended to negate the person of Christ and His power (the gospel) in our lives.

Strongholds in the Head

Mable had bought the lie of the fear of others (Proverbs 29:25). Her fear ensnared her to a life of mental bondage, as manifested through people-pleasing, peer pressure, worry, and anxiety. She was overly concerned about what others thought about her. She was hyper-focused on virtually everything about herself. She second-guessed her thoughts, questions, and concerns. She doubted her choices and actions. She anxiously controlled how she looked in public and what she wore. Satanic forces could not destroy her soul (Plan A), but they could influence her mind until her usefulness in making God's name great was marginalized (Plan B). Taking every evil argument captive and making it bow to the name of Jesus was an illusionary, theological pipe dream. God is the truth, and His purpose for coming to this world was to transform you so you could walk in His truth. The devil's job is to disrupt the truth God provides by motivating you to believe a lie. He hopes to set up deceitful strongholds—mental arguments—in your mind.

I have no greater joy than to hear that my children are walking in the truth.

(3 John 1:4)

When the Spirit of truth comes, he will guide you into all the truth.

(John 16:13)

Sanctify them in the truth; your word is truth.

(John 17:17)

Our Common Lies

What lies keep the gospel from dominating your thought life? What strongholds have been set up in your mind that hinder the sanctifying work of God in your life? What sinful thought fortresses reside in your head?

1. **LIES YOU TELL YOURSELF:** I have to be perfect, I must be happy, and I need people to agree with me. I cannot shake my past, and I deserve better than this.
2. **LIES THE WORLD TELLS YOU:** I must be true to myself. I am number one. I am only human; everybody makes mistakes.
3. **LIES YOU SAY IN YOUR MARRIAGE:** It is your fault. If only I had not married you. You make me so mad. Why can't you be like so and so? I wish I were like so and so.
4. **LIES THAT DISTORT THE GOSPEL:** I must earn God's love. God will not protect me. God does not love me. I can do what I want; God will forgive me. If I were more spiritual, I would not struggle like this. God will bless me if I obey.
5. **LIES FROM THE QUESTIONS WE ASK:** Does God really hear me? Does God really love me? Has God abandoned me? Why does God not stop the pain?

When these types of thought-fortress lies continue to roll around in our heads, they will take our minds into captivity and move us out of line with the gospel (Galatians 2:14). Outside gospel lines will ultimately reduce Jesus to become less than what He should be, and the Spirit's power in our lives will be reduced to less than what it can be.

Fighting with God's Truth

It is essential that you arm yourself with God's truth to overcome these strongholds—these thought fortresses. You cannot arm yourself with fleshly weapons. If you do, you may feel as though you have won the battle, but there will be more lies heaped upon the original lies. Fleshly weapons come from our human strength. Here are a few human weapons that are commonly used to fight the lies listed:

Adultery	Alcohol	Anger
Anxiety	Bitterness	Education
Exercise	Gossip	Medication
Porn	Self-righteousness	Shopping
Unforgiveness	Weight Gain	Worry

There are plenty more. You will notice how not all of these things are necessarily bad. It is bad when you use them as a means to feel better about yourself or to pull yourself out of the dumps while not living in the freedom and power the gospel provides. Ultimately, these things will not work. They will further enslave you while creating more ongoing dysfunction in your relationships. Spiritual warfare looks different. It contextualizes itself in the gospel—the person and work of Jesus Christ—on your behalf. He is the one you need to cooperate with regarding the battle for your mind. I am going to take each lie noted and pull it through a gospel filter. I am going to lay the gospel hammer on it, to crush its head (Genesis 3:15), which I hope will be the beginning of your journey to take your thoughts captive.

Defeating the Lie

1. **LIES YOU TELL YOURSELF:** *I have to be perfect.* You do not have to be perfect. In fact, if you try to be perfect, you will be rejecting the righteousness of Christ, while choosing to hold up your righteousness as the answer. Not accepting Christ's righteousness is another gospel—the gospel of self-atonement. Not admitting the truth of your imperfection makes you a liar (1 John 1:8).

2. **LIES THE WORLD TELLS YOU:** *You must be true to yourself.* You must be faithful to Christ. He is the one you live for, not for yourself. Living for yourself is the lie of the world—a self-centered, anti-Christ way of thinking. You are to die to yourself while fully trusting Christ, who knows better than you do.

3. **LIES YOU SAY IN YOUR MARRIAGE:** *It is your fault/I deserve better.* You will never be happy if things always go your way. You will implode through your insatiable imbibing of self-centeredness. You are called to be content as you learn how to be sufficient through Christ rather than your personal preferences or what may even be good desires (Philippians 4:11-13).

4. **LIES THAT DISTORT THE GOSPEL:** *I must earn God's love/God won't protect me.* Jesus Christ died for you on the cross. He, who was in the form of God, took on the form of a servant to rescue you. There is no greater love than a man who will lay down his

life for another person. (Read Philippians 2:5-11, Romans 5:6-9, and John 15:13.)

5. **LIES FROM THE QUESTIONS WE ASK:** *Does God really hear me?* The answer is similar to number four, except we want to add a proper theology of suffering. We are called to suffer, but if we equate suffering to God distancing Himself, we will not be able to understand God the way we should (1 Peter 2:18-25).

Time to Fight

Mable's battles were not primarily against the people in her world. Sure—her daddy did give her a raw deal. She also had bad things happen to her from others. Her battles go much deeper than the things done to her. Mable is in a spiritual battle with the evil influences of this evil world. When Satan tempted Christ, there would not have been a temptation if Satan could not deliver on what he was offering. Your temptations come when evil demonic forces influence your desires, and the temptation is real because they can give you your evil desires. When your desires cooperate with evil influences, you can rest assured that a stronghold will develop in your mind. When those lies take your mind captive, your body will follow suit. When you immerse your life mainly in the things of this world and its influences, you will be coerced, controlled, and captured by the things of this world—and that warfare will situate itself in your mind.

A gospel-informed mental warrior can quickly take renegade thoughts captive to obey Christ. But you must take the battle in you seriously because your enemy most certainly takes it seriously. You must be influenced more by the Spirit to desire the things of God. It is also essential that you surround yourself with people who can help you in this battle for your mind.

Call to Action

1. What lies do you believe?
2. Have your beliefs developed into strongholds?
3. What has been the fallout from such strongholds?
4. What is one thing you know you can change right now?
5. Who will you enlist to help destroy these strongholds?

5

Stinking Thinking

The noetic effect of sin means our thinking can be stinking at times. Humans, born in the image of God, fell into sin. Our fall broke the purity and clarity of the mind that God gave to us. We need a change of mind, which the mind map in this chapter will help us to understand.

After the fall, humanity became a walking dichotomy: God's perfect creation but distorted in every way, including our minds. Part of what alienation from God means is that our minds are not right. Just because a person may know who God is, it does not mean his thinking is in line with God. The worst case of this in Scripture is the Devil and demons (James 2:19). Knowing God does not guarantee that our thoughts will lead to the right faith (Romans 10:16). Even after we become regenerated and are made right with God, our thinking continues to lag behind our identity in Christ. The doctrine of progressive sanctification implies that our thinking will become more and more in line with how God thinks. The implication is our thinking is still not completely right, but can evolve incrementally.

> For although they knew God, they did not honor him as God or give thanks to him, but they became futile in their thinking, and their foolish hearts were darkened.
>
> (Romans 1:21)

Noetic Effect

The noetic effect of sin means our minds were darkened, futile, and foolish. Paul knew this, as we see in Romans 1:21. We also see him giving us some practical advice on how to overcome this problem in Philippians 4:8 by laying out a format to help us change our thinking. Most Christians know their thinking is off-center—not completely in line with God's Word. I am not sure how aware they are of the depth of their depravity or how to correct their condition. The goal for them—and us—is to recalibrate our inferior Bible knowledge and the application of that knowledge. The more accurate we are with our theology and its proper application, the more holy we can be, the more sound we will think, and the more harmony we will experience with others.

While correct biblical knowledge and application are not everything, they are big things. We adjust and correct our practical faith in proportion to how we think about God and His Word. In a typical counseling session, part of my job is to help a person correct poor biblical thinking. They may know God, but they might be unaware of how various negative shaping influences have altered their thinking. I'm not only talking about the foundational shaping influence of being in Adam but also many shaping influences that have developed their minds before and after salvation.

The most obvious influence is the person's parents or guardians. Other authorities are their genetic capacities and competencies, like IQ and DNA. Additionally, most of the people that I have counseled had negative relational and religious experiences. Sadly, religion has one of the most potent and adverse effects on a person who struggles with poor theological thinking.

Fearful Unbelieving

One of the most potent shaping influences is fear. Fear is the most oft-repeated appeal in the Word of God. The Lord does not want us to live in fear. He knows we're susceptible to fear's encroachments, and one of the common ways a person fears is about God, e.g., their confidence in God's Word regarding their salvation. Believers can genuinely doubt whether God has saved them. This debilitating tension is because their hearts were darkened, futile, and foolish. Then, God saved them. But as children of God, their minds were not perfected. They may not have learned how to apply the perfect righteousness that they received from Christ.

In such cases, their thinking needs to be changed and brought in line with the Word of God, the new authority over their minds. To help with that, I have created a fictional case study about a person who doubted his salvation. His name is Biff. In addition to questioning his salvation, Biff came to me struggling with depression and despair. The more we talked, the more I realized these were symptoms of a deeper problem. Underneath the depression was a heart of fear. But that was not the bottom of his struggles. With a few more directed questions and extended conversations, it became apparent that Biff had a culprit that motivated his fear. Biff was an unbelieving believer (Mark 9:24). Biff was not confident that God was satisfied with him.

Biff's Approval Drive

Biff came from a legalistic religious culture. It was a fear-based culture of do's and don'ts, lists, and rules. He was a rule-based practitioner of his religion with a genuine love for God, but he never could shake his poor theological premise of law-keeping. He layered his religious experience on top of a poor relationship with his father, which served as a pre-existing condition. Biff's dad was quiet in speech and passive in action but never withheld his displeasure from his son when he felt Biff needed a stern lecture. Biff interacted with his dad very little unless he messed up, which is when he "got fussed at." Experiencing love, grace, mercy, patience, and appreciation from another human being was a foreign idea for Biff. He brought this type of thinking into his rule-based religious experience. As you might suspect, being part of a religious movement that valued performance was perfect for Biff.

Though his dad never appreciated him, his religious culture did. In this new environment, Biff excelled in all the things they asked him to do. Through the preaching of the Word, he received a steady diet of rules and regulations, which he digested and imitated with zeal. The more rules that he obeyed, the more he felt appreciated. They told him what Bible to read, what kinds of clothes to wear, what types of music to listen to, what places were acceptable to go, what books were permissible, and what churches were approved to attend. He loved it. It worked. He was right with God and man. All he had to do was subscribe to their prescribed lists. Biff's religion was ready-made for a person who had a strong desire to please.

Internal Awkwardness

And he was a quick study. He figured out the ropes and became a top-notch performer in his religious circle—but something was missing. Internally, Biff knew his thinking was off-center. As he read verses about how his relationship with God was not based on his works, he became confused (Titus 3:5). Though his religious culture affirmed a non-works, all of grace teaching, it was clear to him that what he did or did not do mattered more. He told me,

> How could my works not matter to God when they were the raw materials for having any type of

relationship with my religious friends? If I watched the wrong movie, listened to unapproved music, or went to a bad church, my approval rating among my friends tanked.

Without seeking to understand me or help me, they judged me and began to distance themselves from me. If I did conform to my Christian culture's preferences, I could enter back into their good graces. If I did not, they would shun me because they said I was a dangerous influence on their friends. Then they would tag me with the "L" word, and I don't mean legalist. I was a liberal. It is so hard to understand. Does God grade me this way? My friends were like my dad, and I began to think God was this way, too.

It was not long before Biff's relationship with God grew cold. In time, he chucked his religion altogether and began living a liberal, licentious lifestyle. His religious friends did what he expected them to do: they judged him and then promptly separated from him. According to their legalistic calculating, it was a justified response because they warned him.

A Crisis in Faith

What his friends did not understand was their religion pushed Biff toward his crisis of faith. In Biff's mind, his father, religion, friends, and God were all the same: right behavior was a condition for a relationship.

- His dad made it clear: right behavior is a condition for a relationship.
- His religion made it clear: right behavior is a condition for a relationship.
- He assumed God would only love him if he behaved a certain way.

For by grace you have been saved through faith. And this is not your own doing; it is the gift of God, not a result of works, so that no one may boast.

(Ephesians 2:8-9)

By the time Biff came to me, he was spiritually distant, angry, and cynical. From Biff's stunted perspective, God was on the sidelines. Trust was not a possibility. It was a trifecta of rejection: religion, family, and God—all based on his performance. Biff was depressed and discouraged. He had lost hope. We spent hours hammering out a new theology. Though he came to me outwardly distant, it became apparent that he wanted help. He was in search of the true and living God. He needed a change of mind.

Mind Mapping Salvation

Finally, brothers, whatever is true, whatever is honorable, whatever is just, whatever is pure, whatever is lovely, whatever is commendable, if there is any excellence, if there is anything worthy of praise, think about these things.

(Philippians 4:8)

I wanted Biff to change his mind about God's acceptance of him. I wanted him to see that it was not based on his behavior but on the behavior of Jesus Christ. Biff's behavior would never merit a proper and pleasing relationship with the Father, but Christ's works would. I hoped Biff would understand the gospel practically. During one of our initial counseling sessions, I began to map out Philippians 4:8 for Biff. I wanted him to practically see how to move from stinking thinking to biblical thinking. You can follow the process laid out in the mind map with any bad thoughts you have. Here are the steps I mapped out for Biff.

Thoughts: What is your unbiblical thought? What is it about your thinking that needs a biblical adjustment? Write it on a piece of paper. I noted his response at the top of the mind map, which has the words "My Thoughts." The particular thought that I'm interacting with for Biff in this mind map is whether Biff is a Christian. You can run any thought through the Philippians 4:8 filter.

Filter: Once you have established the thought you want to address, you must see if it fits any of Paul's six categories: Is it true, honorable, just, pure, lovely, or commendable? An unbiblical thought will not make it through this filter. To press your idea all the way down the mind map, you must align your thinking according to the Word of God.

Scripture: For Biff, I gave him verses that were true, honorable, just, pure, lovely, and commendable regarding his salvation. There were seventeen verses or passages altogether. His thought of losing his salvation was none of the ideas that Paul was teaching. The seventeen verses or passages spoke to Biff's salvation, getting saved, how to be born again, who regenerates you, and what the Lord requires for salvation. All of the verses affirm that you cannot lose your salvation; it is not based on a believer's works, but it is a total reliance on the actions of another. Because Scripture is the authority through which we filter our thoughts, Biff had a new way of thinking. All of the verses were either right, honorable, just, pure, lovely, or commendable. This kind of biblical thinking was a far cry from how Biff had been thinking.

Excellent and Worthy: Based on the authority of God's Word, Biff had something to think of that was excellent and worthy of praise.

Think: As you can see, Biff moved from the top of the map with his wrong thinking to the bottom. He began to push through the Philippians 4:8 grid, and as he did, his thinking began to adjust according to God's Word.

By the time he reached the bottom of the page, his thoughts had changed from how Adam had shaped them because of the fall, bad parenting, and poor religion to a new kind of shape by the Word of God. He repented of his stinking thinking and began to think like an informed biblicist. You can do this too. If you're not familiar with God's Word, it may serve you to find someone who is, so they can help you adjust whatever thoughts need changing. If you are comfortable enough to do this alone, go for it. My appeal is that you share how God is changing your thinking.

Call to Action

1. What are some common thought patterns in your life that do not align with God's Word? How have these thoughts shaped your emotions and actions?

2. Have you ever doubted God's acceptance of you? What biblical truths can you meditate on to combat this kind of unbelief?

3. Like Biff, have past shaping influences—family, religious experiences, or culture—distorted your understanding of God's grace? How can you begin renewing your mind with Scripture?

4. When faced with a wrong thought, do you know how to filter it through Philippians 4:8? What steps can you take to practice this kind of biblical thinking daily?

5. Who in your life can help you identify and correct wrong thinking? Will you seek counsel from a mature believer to help you grow in your understanding of God's truth?

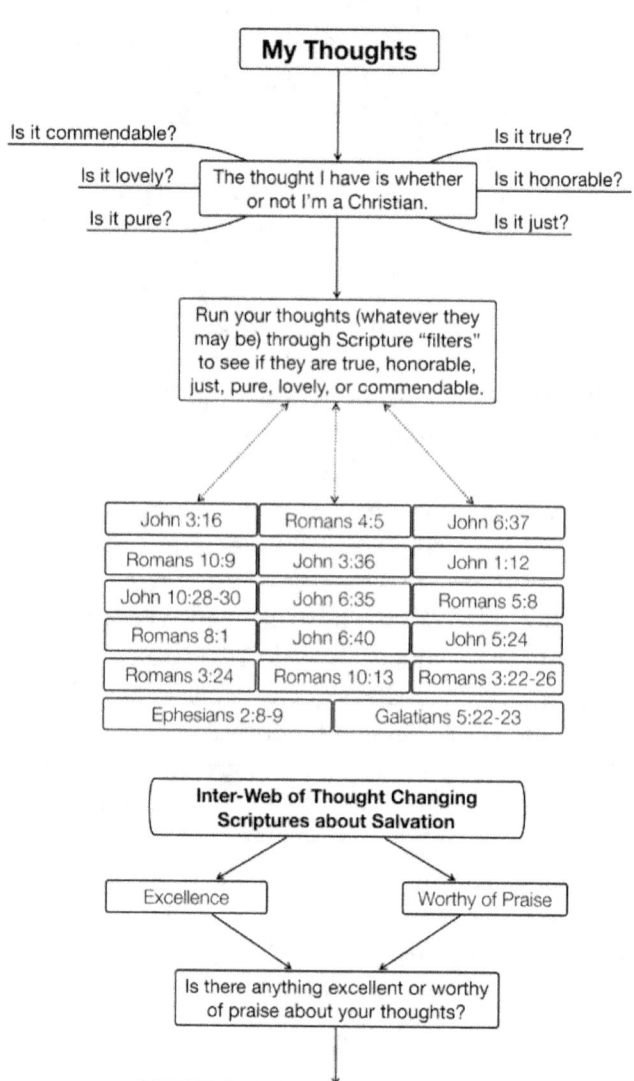

Mind Mapping Thoughts with a Philippians 4:8 Filter

Finally, brothers, whatever is true, whatever is honorable, whatever is just, whatever is pure, whatever is lovely, whatever is commendable, if there is any excellence, if there is anything worthy of praise, think about these things.

My Thoughts

Is it commendable?   Is it true?

Is it lovely?   The thought I have is whether   Is it honorable?
                or not I'm a Christian.
Is it pure?   Is it just?

Run your thoughts (whatever they may be) through Scripture "filters" to see if they are true, honorable, just, pure, lovely, or commendable.

John 3:16	Romans 4:5	John 6:37
Romans 10:9	John 3:36	John 1:12
John 10:28-30	John 6:35	Romans 5:8
Romans 8:1	John 6:40	John 5:24
Romans 3:24	Romans 10:13	Romans 3:22-26
Ephesians 2:8-9		Galatians 5:22-23

Inter-Web of Thought Changing Scriptures about Salvation

Excellence   Worthy of Praise

Is there anything excellent or worthy of praise about your thoughts?

NOW, I CAN THINK ON THE RIGHT THING

6

Change Your Thoughts

If your life was put in three different file drawers that represented your past, present, and future, which of the file drawers drains the most joy out of your life? For example, if there is a disruption of your contentment, it would indicate something has gone wrong in—at least—one of your file drawers. Thus, you would identify the problem and begin to restore contentment by isolating the issue and initiating a process to bring the gospel to bear on what seeks to disrupt your mind. To help drill down into this concept, I have developed three mind maps to bring clarity to taking our rogue thoughts captive.

Circularity of Thoughts

For where your treasure is, there your heart will be also.

(Matthew 6:21)

It is impossible not to think about something. Your mind is a busy street of thoughts that runs continuously through your waking hours. Your thoughts have so much power over you that they form random, willy-nilly mental collages even while you are asleep. We call this dreaming. Because God made you in His image, you can think, ponder, and reflect. Because of what happened in Genesis 3, you can think, ponder, and reflect poorly, even to the detriment of your soul. There is a circularity between your thoughts and your point of focus—as the mind map below points out. Your thoughts makeup what has captured your focus, and what you focus on captures your thoughts.

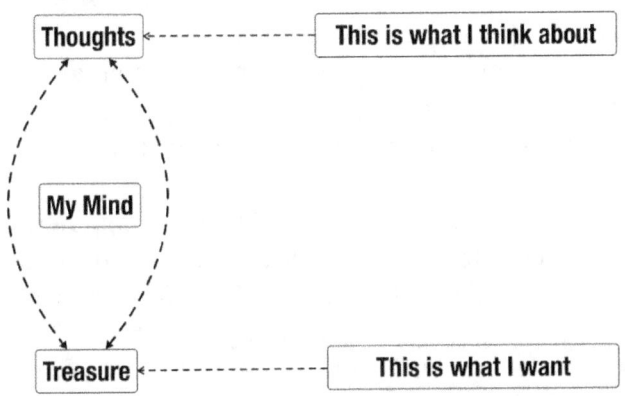

The Circularity of Thought

Finally, brothers, whatever is true, whatever is honorable, whatever is just, whatever is pure, whatever is lovely, whatever is commendable, if there is any excellence, if there is anything worthy of praise, think about these things (Philippians 4:8).

Thoughts ← - - - - - - - - - - - This is what I think about

My Mind

Treasure ← - - - - - - - - - - This is what I want

For where your treasure is, there your heart will be also Matthew 6:20).

There could be the chicken and the egg discussion here as far as what came first—the thought or the treasure—though it does not matter. What matters is that you must address both your thought life and the things you value. The blessing of the circularity of *thought-to-treasure* is that if your treasure is right, your thoughts will be right. If you are pursuing the right things, your thoughts will be vital benefits to you. The bane of this circularity is when your treasure is not the right thing. If so, over time, your thoughts will have drifted so far from being in line with the gospel that it will take an act of God and the community of faith to restore you to a sound way of thinking.

> *The key to renewing your mind is learning to live more and more in focused mode rather than default mode. The discontented person has kicked the brain into neutral, which leads to the default mode.*
> – Charlie Boyd

If a joyful spirit is not how others characterize you, or if you are not living in regular, uninterrupted contentment, you must reassess your *thought-to-treasure* construct.

> *Have you realized that most of your unhappiness in life is due to the fact that you are listening to yourself instead of talking to yourself? Take those thoughts that come to you the moment you wake up in the morning. You have not originated them, but they start talking to you, they bring back the problems of yesterday, etc. Somebody is talking. Who is talking to you? Your self is talking to you.*
> – D. Martyn Lloyd-Jones, Spiritual Depression

This insight supports Paul's appeal to think about the right things and do the right thing. Martin-Jones' statement demonstrates the circularity of *thought-to-treasure*. What you think about is what you want, and what you want is your thought life. The question to ponder is, "Do you want the right things?" Are there things that you want to be true, honorable, just, pure, lovely, and commendable? These six words make up a rich person's treasure. If you want these things, you have the right treasure. You value the right stuff. If your treasure is un- or sub-biblical, your thoughts will be lacking, and the contentment you desire will drain from your soul.

Controlling Your Thoughts

There was a time when Paul did not properly control his thoughts. Thinking well is a learned behavior, which is what he was teaching the Philippians. Eventually, Paul learned how to experience joy-filled contentment in his thoughts.

> Not that I am speaking of being in need, for I have learned in whatever situation I am to be content. I know how to be brought low, and I know how to abound. In any and every circumstance, I have learned the secret of facing plenty and hunger, abundance and need.
> (Philippians 4:11-12)

There is no denying that retraining your thought life will take much work over an extended period. Resetting the general direction of your thinking is not a five-step program but a complete change of perspective. The Christian life is not so much about a roadmap but a compass. It is not about steps that you can map out to be a content-filled Christian. The Christian life is the predetermined setting of your compass on the gospel, and then training yourself to have joyful contentment in this new direction for living. The truest, most honorable, just, pure, lovely, and commendable things that you can do practically is live out the two great commandments (Matthew 22:36-40). No other kind of life on earth transcends a person's tenacious desire to love God and others most of all. All other attempts to fill the void in our souls will fail. Inward, self-focused thinking depreciates happiness. Life is found in God, not in ourselves. The person who is fixated on God while doing the things that God does—serving others—will flourish in this life and enjoy great rewards in the one to come.

Changing Your Thoughts

Learning contentment comes from intentionally and joyfully focusing your thoughts on being grateful for the people that God has brought into your life while caring about their interests above your own (Philippians 2:3-4). One of the most life-giving and self-filling questions you could ever ask another person is, "How may I serve you?" When this kind of thinking becomes your treasure, your thoughts will gradually move from discontentedness to contentedness. What I am talking about here is a gospel vision that the Lord gives. If discontentment is the issue, there is not much you can do until you see the need and are motivated to change while pleading with the Lord to bring change to your thought life.

- Do you want joy?
- Would you like to find lasting contentment?
- How desperate are you?

She said to Jacob, "Give me children, or I shall die!"
(Genesis 30:1)

The Circularity of Thought

For where your treasure is, there your heart will be also (Matthew 6:20).

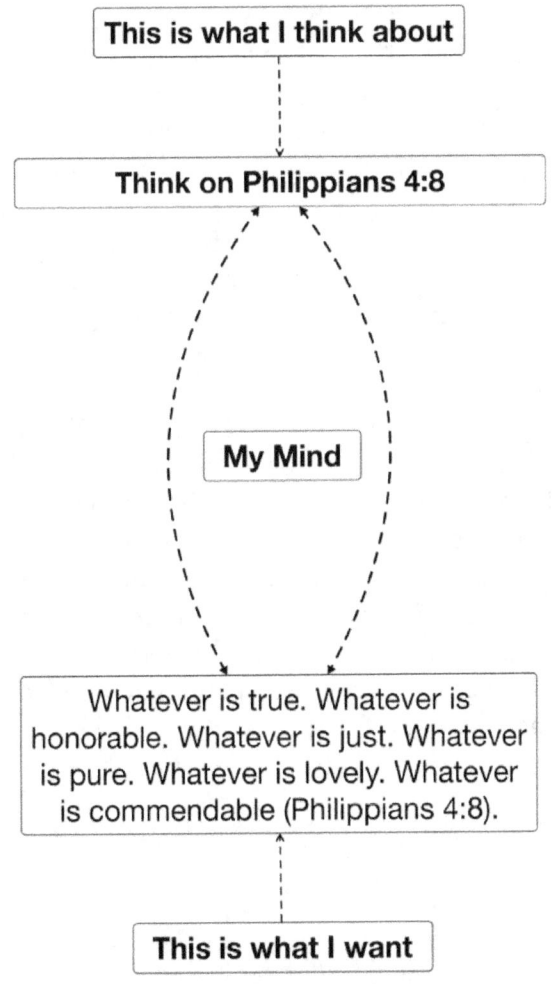

This is what I think about

Think on Philippians 4:8

My Mind

Whatever is true. Whatever is honorable. Whatever is just. Whatever is pure. Whatever is lovely. Whatever is commendable (Philippians 4:8).

This is what I want

A contented life will come after you decide you will not be satisfied with any other kind of life. It reminds me of Rachel's desperate plea for children. I am not altogether sure of her motives, but I am sure of her desperation. Learning contentment is born out of a desperate and intentional heart. Your peace will come in proportion to your dissatisfaction with any traces of selfishness in your life. Intention guides your attention. Or, as Jesus said, "Where your treasure is, there will be your heart also." The question becomes, "Is your primary goal to pursue God and others for the joy-filled expectation of finding your fullest contentment through Him while serving others?" This transition will require a mental fight every day of your life. Each day, you will have to take your thoughts captive because your thought life will be relentless in derailing your mind, with the hope of keeping you off your impassioned Christ-centered trajectories (2 Corinthians 10:3-6).

> The eye is the lamp of the body. So, if your eye is healthy, your whole body will be full of light, but if your eye is bad, your whole body will be full of darkness. If then the light in you is darkness, how great is the darkness! No one can serve two masters, for either he will hate the one and love the other, or he will be devoted to the one and despise the other. You cannot serve God and money.
>
> (Matthew 6:22-24)

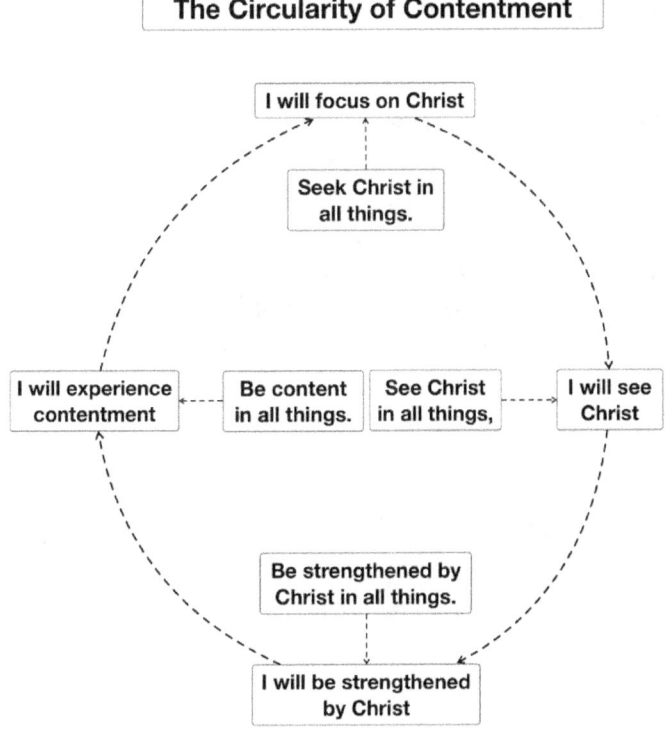

The Circularity of Contentment

Which will it be, because you can only have one? You cannot serve two masters. What are you seeking? What you pursue is what you see, and what you see is what you are chasing. What do you see? Where have you set your truest affections?

Set your minds on things that are above, not on things that are on earth.

(Colossians 3:2)

If you make your aim to seek and to know Christ, over time, you will begin to see Christ in all the things that happen to you, and you will receive from Christ the strength to be content in every circumstance. Paul saw Christ as his chief aspiration and joy in his life (Philippians 3:8-10). Paul's focus on Christ was a learned behavior. Through this intentional focus, he received the strength he needed to be content, regardless of all the circumstances in which he found himself (Philippians 4:11-12).

Seek Christ in all things,
see Christ in all things,
be strengthened by Christ in all things,
to be content in all things.

Call to Action

If your life was put in three different file drawers that represented your past, present, and future, which of the file drawers drains the most joy out of your life? Your first call to action is to determine if discontentment generally characterizes you.

- Would you consider yourself a God-sustained, joy-filled person? If so, why? If not, why?

Remember Paul's comprehensive de facto qualifier: I have learned to be content in whatever situation I am in (Philippians 4:11). I am asking a comprehensive question—past, present, and future, not a micro question where you can pick a slice of your life. God's contentment should be like breathing; no matter where you go or who you are with, you are content.

- Have you learned that regardless of the circumstance or the context, you are the happy recipient of the good Lord's ongoing contentment?
- If this is not the normal condition of your soul, which file drawer would you say disrupts your contentment? Is it your unresolved past, your unsettling present, or your uncertain future?

After you narrow down the file drawer question, you can begin to examine what you want that you are not getting. If your soul is in turmoil, your greatest treasure is not Christ but something else—something you are not able to control or secure. Here are ten examples of things that tempt us to want more than Christ. All of these statements begin with, "I am not content because..."

- My marriage is not what I want it to be.
- My life has not turned out the way I had hoped.
- I do not have all the things I desire.
- I am not living like my friends.
- My children are not the way I want them to be.
- I struggle with fear, comparison, self-pity, or anger.
- I am not married.
- I am married but to the wrong kind of person.
- The Lord will not give me what I want.
- I want, I want, I want, I want, but cannot have.

Any of these things can supplant Christ as your greatest treasure. If you have not discovered how to have a comprehensive contentment in Christ that spans every facet of your life, there is another treasure competing for your heart. If that is true, I want you to do the following seven things.

1. Pray through this chapter, asking the Lord to identify what is wrong.
2. Reflect on what the Spirit of God reveals to you.
3. Write those reflections down so you can own them. Make them yours.
4. Commit your life to change what the Lord has identified that needs changing about yourself.
5. Share these reflections with a few friends—at least one trusted friend.
6. Walk out what you are learning, making sure your friend walks with you.
7. Review these things until you have a new and learned behavior.

7

Memories

Our memories can play tricks on our minds, and if we're not careful, we can grow dissatisfied with our lives while giving too much thought to a past that was not how we had hoped. We may even revise our past—unwittingly— to fit a narrative we prefer. Learning how to capture these uninvited, rogue memories and submit them to Christ's obedience is crucial. Let me illustrate what I mean with my friend, Biff.

Biff and Mable

Biff had an active sexual life during college. One of his relationships lasted for two years. Her name was Marge. Many people assumed that Biff would marry Marge. After he graduated and took a job in another city, his pace of life picked up, and Marge slowly drifted from his mind and his life. Enter Mable. Once he settled into his new career and apartment and became more of a local, he eventually began to think about companionship again. Mable was a colleague, and though he was initially turned off by her, being with her each day softened his heart.

Mable liked him from the beginning and was persistent in her sly way about getting that first date. Biff did not have a long line of girls seeking him out, so he went on another date with Mable. And then another, and another. Though he wasn't that interested in her, it was something to do, and she was a girl who liked him, which was a plus. Before long, people were making assumptions about Biff and Mable. Biff didn't mind. He loved the idea of romance and fun because it brought back memories of the good old days, a carefree time. Living in an apartment alone never appealed to Biff anyway. So, he hung out with Mable. Soon, they became inseparable. He even started liking her.

Five Years Later

Biff and Mable were married. They stayed in their careers and worked long hours. They eventually bought a fixer-upper. They put off having children, saying they were not ready for the next big step. Unbeknownst to Mable, Biff's commitment to her was not that deep. He "loved" her but was more committed to his job than his wife. The sweet things he initially liked about Mable became annoyances, but because of his lack of commitment, he could mostly shrug off the disappointments and irritants. Besides, he had a fall-back plan. He loved his career and was on the rise—a promising new star in his company. Deep down, though, he was not happy. It is one thing to date, but he never realized the commitment and ever-present expectations of marriage. Even with all of the good things coming his way through his job, there was a growing emptiness along with a desire for less attachment to Mable. Biff was set up for a struggle.

Memories

- He had a superficial commitment to his wife.
- Without a deep commitment, there was a magnification of her annoyances.
- His job was fun but not satisfying.
- Because he broke off his relationship with Marge due to the move, her perfect ways remained alluring.

Biff was a Christian, and he knew even though he was self-centered, God was somewhere in his mess, and it was wrong to struggle the way he did. So he went to his pastor to get help for the secret thoughts that he could not shake. He gave his pastor the scoop about his marriage, and his pastor began to address some of the significant areas in his life that needed to change.

Frozen in Time

Often, when a person dies younger than expected, that person can become fixed in time as a perfect individual. JFK was such a person. His life was cut short, and to many people, he is one of those near-perfect American icons. People ignore his womanizing and poor politics. He was on the move, up and coming, and then suddenly, by an assassin's bullet, time froze him tragically. Because of his death and a lack of technology and media discretion that prohibited the telling of the whole story of JFK, many remember him as a somewhat perfect, iconic person. That happens when we freeze an individual in time, and their true selves do not become known or popularized. Marge was like this to Biff. Because of their innocuous break-up and permanent separation, she was his frozen-in-time lover.

They had a fun-filled relationship that was problem-free because they were in college, drinking in the party scene, rocking out at football games, and enjoying timely breaks from each other. Biff had his life, and Marge had hers. They came together for two to six hours a day, but not every day, and when they did come together, they had fun. The life he lived with Marge was an artificial relational world that was suited to selfish people. The life he lives with Mable is real life with no breaks. With Marge, it was fantasyland. With Mable, it is reality. Biff finds it more comfortable to live in his imagination than his current circumstances. And because he terminated his relationship with Marge, they did not go the distance by entering into the challenges of relationship building through marriage. Thus, all of his memories are good—frozen in time, which is why they are so appealing.

If he truly understood the doctrine of sin, he would know that Marge is a sinner, too. Just because what they did as friends and how they went about doing it did not challenge their relationship, it does not mean Marge is the better gal. Both Marge and Mable, along with Biff, are sinners. It's not as perfect as he would like to believe. This scenario is the temptation with many couples in troubled marriages or marriages struggling due to past romantic memories. They either think about a previous relationship or dream about a future one and begin to believe that the grass is greener in the past or the future. They willingly blind themselves to the statistical reality that second and third marriages are more likely to end in divorce than their first one. In such cases, their view of sin is corrupted by their lust for self-centered relational gratification.

Lack of Aggression

Whenever a person struggles with past thoughts, in the way that Biff was, it's a sure-fire clue that there is a lack of aggressive, other-centeredness in the current relationship. Biff's pastor pointed this out to him. Biff knew it, but he was not willing to be honest about how he presented his thought life to his pastor. He liked Marge better because of how she made him feel. Let's consider the gospel for a minute. Suppose Christ picked who He wanted to be with based on how the person made Him feel (Romans 5:8). If so, there would be no gospel. He would be like all the other gods from all the different religions: we would have to earn His love because there is nothing attractive about us.

Biff's marriage is like all the other religions: his wife has to win his heart rather than Biff winning his wife's heart. The gospel is the opposite of how Biff functions in his marriage. Christ won our hearts rather than expecting us to make Him happy first. Christ had intentional, relational aggression because it was not primarily about what He could get out of the relationship but what He could pour into it, which is not how Biff thinks. "I know, I know," he says, "I love Mable." To a degree and in his own way, he does. But he does not love her according to the gospel, which is why her annoyances are so annoying to him.

- He has forgotten that Marge is a sinner, too.
- He has forgotten how Christ loved him.

Our minds do not make us victims, holding us captive. We choose what we put into them. Biff centers his mind on a fantasy that satisfies him while he lives with a woman who cannot compete with his memories. (What he is doing is the essence and the snare of pornography. Porn is mostly a fantasy world of the mind, where perfect people with ideal bodies perform for the willing addict.) Biff has not been careful with his thought life. He finds himself slipping into that fantasy world, even during company meetings. As time goes by, he grows in his disdain for the real people in his real world, especially the imperfect ones who are the closest to him. This snare is why Biff needs to shake himself violently while reorienting his mind back to the gospel.

> Do nothing from selfish ambition or conceit, but in humility count others more significant than yourselves.
>
> (Philippians 2:3)

Biff has set up rivals in his mind: Marge and Mable. The former one he likes and the latter one he is growing to resent. The bad news here is that the latter one is his wife. He needs to repent. One of the ways he can change his mind is by reading the rest of the Philippians text, which talks about how the gospel came to become just like us to save us from our sins (Philippians 2:5-11). Biff needs to spend every day of his life asking the Father to purge his mind of self-centered thinking and to give him affection for his wife. He needs to fall in love with his wife the right way. The only way he can do this is by first coming to terms with the gospel.

Historical Revision

Our thoughts are not as accurate as we might want to believe. We skew our perspectives, especially when we revisit the past. How many times have you been with a friend, recounting history, and someone who happened to live that experience with you had a different perspective than you? We should approach the historical moments in our lives with humility. Let me make two simple statements—universal truths—to help you get your mind around this idea of historical revision:

- **WE ARE NOT OMNISCIENT:** Though this might be disarming, it is true. You do not know all there is to know. Only God knows everything. Biff thinks things would have been different with Marge. Biff is wrong—dead wrong. Biff and Marge are sinners. There would have been dysfunction in their relationship if they were married.
- **WE ARE NOT INFALLIBLE:** We are fallible with all of our thoughts. We view things through a skewed lens, and we will always skew our lens to our advantage. Because we seek our advantage, don't you think it is possible that we will misinterpret the past to our advantage? We are loyalists who are loyal to ourselves—our self-centered realism affects what we believe about our past.

I remember many years ago having a conversation with my brother about our childhood. It was interesting to hear his perspective. At one moment in our conversation, I thought to myself, "Was he even in my childhood?" The way he talked about our life together and the way I thought about our life together were, at times, not on the same planet. Here's the point: Biff needs to hold his past humbly and with suspicion. The humble heart holds things loosely, while the proud heart is inflexible. Being rigid about your past thoughts can lead you into mental bondage and relational conflict.

The Will of God

The only way you can know God's will with absolute assurance is by looking in the rearview mirror. You cannot completely understand God's will for the future, but you can know it by looking at what has happened.

> Come now, you who say, "Today or tomorrow we will go into such and such a town and spend a year there and trade and make a profit"—yet you do not know what tomorrow will bring. Instead, you ought to say, "If the Lord wills, we will live and do this or that." As it is, you boast in your arrogance. All such boasting is evil. So whoever knows the right thing to do and fails to do it, for him it is sin.
>
> (James 4:13-17)

The future is opaque, but the past is clear, and we now know that God wanted Biff to marry Mable. How do we know this? Because he did marry her. I do not know all the particulars regarding how he came to that decision, but I do know he came to it, and that is God's will for his life. Dreaming, hoping, thinking, and maybe even strategizing about another relationship is arrogance and a blatant dismissal of God's will for Biff's life. He needs to know this, and he needs to respond to the Lord through full-throated, humble repentance.

> So whoever knows the right thing to do and fails to
> do it, for him it is sin.
>
> (James 4:17)

If he will humble himself to these truths and pursue God and his wife, he will begin to experience a change in his thought life (Matthew 22:36-40). He will fall in love with her, which starts on his knees, in his closet, as he pleads with the Lord to give him deep affection for Himself, first, and then for Mable. It will be vital for his pastor to address the secret motives of his heart. There will be traces of deception and desires that will keep him hooked on a feeling from his past that he does not want to release to the Lord. Gollum called it his precious in *The Lord of the Rings*. In his heart of hearts, Gollum did not want to let go of the ring of power.

> Finally, brothers, whatever is true, whatever is
> honorable, whatever is just, whatever is pure,
> whatever is lovely, whatever is commendable, if
> there is any excellence, if there is anything worthy
> of praise, think about these things.
>
> (Philippians 4:8)

Call to Action

Biff's story is not unique. Many of us are tempted to revise our past, elevating a memory above our current reality. We deceive ourselves, convincing ourselves that what was left behind is better than what God has given us today. The problem is not our circumstances—it is our self-centered hearts. If you find yourself longing for an idealized past, discontented with the life God has given you, the time for change is now. You must take every thought captive and submit it to Christ's obedience (2 Corinthians 10:5). Will you do the hard work of renewing your mind according to the gospel? Will you choose to love as Christ loves you—not based on fleeting feelings, but on sacrificial commitment? Ask yourself:

1. What are you choosing to dwell on? Are your thoughts shaped by truth or fantasy?
2. Are you holding onto an unrealistic version of the past? Do you need to humbly agree with God that you are not omniscient or infallible in your recollections? Please explain.
3. Are you actively pursuing those relationships in your current sphere? Have you neglected an active, relational aggression—pouring into others rather than expecting them to satisfy you?

God's will for you is not hidden. It is right in front of you. He has placed people in your life for you to love with the same relentless, undeserved love He has given you. You will not fall into biblical love—you must fight for it. That battle begins in your mind, in prayer and repentance, and in the daily choice to think biblically. Will you choose to obey Christ by guarding your thoughts and pursuing love according to the gospel? Or will you continue chasing illusions that will never satisfy? The choice is yours.

8

The Past

Thinking about our past should be a positive time of rejoicing in God's good work in our lives, though, with some folks, it takes work to come to a place of peace about their past. In nearly all counseling contexts, understanding the past is crucial to discern a person's former manner of life and shaping influences that are part of who they are today. Our history is important because God was in our past. (cf. Jeremiah 1:5; Ephesians 1:3-11). His awareness of us did not begin at salvation. Our omniscient and omnipresent God has always been aware of and involved in our lives. He knows more about our past, present, and future than we could ever imagine.

God Was There

Your life is one story—lost and saved—working out for your good and His glory (Romans 8:28). At the beginning and all the way to the end, your life's script comes from the hand of God. He is the author, and you are the participant in the narrative that He is writing. Whether you spent most of your past rebelling against God or following Him, He was there. The good and bad of your life, whether those things happened in your pre- or post-salvation experience, are part of the Lord's sovereign care and design. Becoming born again does not erase what has happened to you, but it does release you from the bondage of what has happened to you (2 Corinthians 5:17).

To be adopted by your heavenly Father is an other-worldly change from what you used to be to what you can be. God adorned you in the garments of redemption. You are eating at the King's table, fully secure in your new lifestyle as God's child—if you are born again (2 Samuel 9:11). For some Christians, the good news of Christ is more theoretical than functional. Because of the horrendous events of these believers' pasts, they struggle with what happened to them. I understand the struggle in their lives. As a two-decade, physically and verbally abused son of an angry drunk who buried two murdered brothers and went through a horrible divorce, I am sympathetic to those who continue to struggle with what happened to them.

Let's Get to Work

Your past can be like a dark shadow that never leaves. It is like living in a world where the sun never shines. This seeming curse is how the past can control a person's present, which has a determining impact on their future. Being born a second time is supposed to have a practical and transformative effect on our lives. God adopted and declared us not guilty of all past, present, and future sins, as well as releasing us from the evil of others. This work is a passive operation that the Lord does to us (Ephesians 2:8-9; Romans 8:1). Our sanctification is different; it is not as passive.

After salvation, God requires you to cooperate with Him in the work He has previously prepared for you. The Lord wants you to participate and enjoy the new relationship with Him. (See Ephesians 2:10; Philippians 2:12-13.) Thus, there is work to do after regeneration (James 2:17). Though this cooperative activity with God is not a condition of your salvation, it is an essential responsibility that affects the quality of your life. This assumption is where your past can be a problem, even crippling your experience with God and others, which is why a struggler needs a new practical theology regarding the past. Part of that theology should include these eight ideas.

1—The Past Is Significant

To put off your old self, which belongs to your former manner of life and is corrupt through deceitful desires.

(Ephesians 4:22)

The psychological culture makes way too much of the past; they see the past as a mystery to be unlocked. There is no biblical warrant for this worldview. The Lord would not lock up your past and then ask you to go on a mysterious field trip to find the secret key to your future sanctification. This concept makes no sense. Conversely, the Christian culture has too easily dismissed the past as though it does not matter, which is also a mistake. Of course, you do not want to be that continual backward-looking Christian who never gains forward momentum in their progressive sanctification. We can live in this tension because Christ connects the quality of our sanctification to who we are in Him, not to who we were in Adam. You have a former manner of life that affects your current manner of life. Paul told the Ephesian Christians that their former way of life impacted their current way of life. He did not ignore what they were before the Lord saved them, and he did not want them to dismiss it lightly.

2—We Are Not Victims

There is a measure of significance to your past, but it should not have controlling power. No person is a helpless victim whose present manner of life is determined by their past manner of life. If your past has more power over you than the grace of God, your thinking about your past is not in line with the gospel. There is a way you are supposed to think about your past, which was Paul's point to them. He had concerns about how a Gentile worldview shaped their thinking. Paul was aware, so he told the Ephesians to be careful about how their past may corrupt their thinking. Carefully read how Paul talked about this.

> Now this I say and testify in the Lord, that you must no longer walk as the Gentiles do, in the futility of their minds. They are darkened in their understanding, alienated from the life of God because of the ignorance that is in them, due to their hardness of heart. They have become callous and have given themselves up to sensuality, greedy to practice every kind of impurity. But that is not the way you learned Christ!
>
> (Ephesians 4:17-20)

3—The Past Affects the Present

Paul was concerned that their thinking might not change. He appealed to the Ephesian converts to no longer walk like the Gentiles, who did so in the futility of their minds. They did this due to ignorance, which meant the Ephesians had not learned Christ the way they should have. They had a darkened understanding that was alienated from the life found in God. The real issue for a person who has been affected by their past is how they are thinking about their past. To be in Christ is a worldview shift. You have come out of darkness, and you are now a child of the light. The number one problem I experience with people who are still affected by their past is they continue to think like they are unbelievers. They do not have a stabilized and maturing faith in God. (See 2 Corinthians 4:6; 2 Peter 3:18; Hebrews 5:11-14.)

4—We Reconstruct the Past

For though we walk in the flesh, we are not waging war according to the flesh. For the weapons of our warfare are not of the flesh but have divine power to destroy strongholds. We destroy arguments and every lofty opinion raised against the knowledge of God, and take every thought captive to obey Christ.

(2 Corinthians 10:3-5)

This point is where it gets interesting for past-dominated Christians. What happened to them by those in their past has more power over them than what is going on with them by God (John 17:17). They live more like fleshly Christians than spiritual Christians. There are arguments from the past that have shaped them. These arguments rise up against the knowledge of God. These thought fortresses control them. The irony is that no person can perfectly interpret or reproduce what has happened to them. Their finiteness and fallenness are conditions that lead them to practice reconstruction. It happens often in counseling.

I will meet with a couple, and one of them will rehearse the weekend's argument with me. Typically, the other spouse jumps in and says, "That's not how it happened." The rebutting spouse is correct. Neither of them can reconstruct their weekend accurately. Their fine-tuned filters and presuppositions disallow them to see the events accurately. They have skewed interpretive filters, tilting toward their unique finite and fallen tendencies. This fact about all of our arguments, in itself, should cause anyone to be suspicious of how they think about what has happened to them.

5—God Was in the Past

The safer way to go is to see our pasts as coming from the Lord for His glory, our good, and the benefit of others. This worldview stabilizes me when I think about my past. I am not a victim of my past but a unique man made in God's image, who the Lord has given a past for His purposes. God knew me before I was born. He brought me into this world through two particular sinners. He carved a path through my past that led me to the cross. It did not matter what kind of sinners my parents were. How could I get from my first birth to my second birth and not be affected by those in my life? It is like we are walking through the world in semi-clean clothes. By the time we get to Jesus Christ, our clothes are filthy rags (Isaiah 64:6). The good news is that God was there, making a path where no path existed, bringing us to His dear Son so we could be born a second time. God was and is with us (Genesis 39:2).

6—Culture Distorts the Past

Unbelievers will try to change their past because that is the only thing they can do. They have a presuppositional lens shaped by a godless worldview. How could they view their past any other way? Their starting point, like ours, determines their ending point. Too many Christians have culturally convoluted thinking about their pasts. They were indoctrinated by worldviews and shaped by influences that have little to do with the Scriptures. If the culture begins by denying the Lord, there is no way they can arrive at God-centered solutions. At the same time, I do not fault the world for doing what it does because that is all it can do. What flummoxes me is how some Christians continue to drink from wells that cannot hold water (Jeremiah 2:13). Nearly all of this confusion about the past is because we have submitted our thoughts to theologies devoid of God and His Word.

7—We Distort the Past

None of us are trustworthy enough to come to infallible conclusions about our pasts. We all should hold a healthy suspicion of ourselves, especially about how we think about what has happened to us. This view is not negative. It is humble self-awareness and wisdom. We cannot be fully aware of our assumptions, values, influences, habits, and blind spots that shape our former manner of life. Paul told the Ephesians believers that their former manner of life was corrupted through deceitful desires. So is ours. We must hold our pasts loosely and not accept that what happened to us is our identity. We are to no longer walk as the Gentiles. We are a new creation, made and shaped by God. Rather than spending our days thinking about what has happened to us, it would be more productive to reflect on how God wants to work in our lives today. Backward fixations will keep us in the grip of our pasts. Forward fixations will change our lives. If we're going to change our past, we must change the only thing we can manage today.

8—Rewrite Your Future

As you incrementally alter your present, you will stand at some future day with a Christ-centered past. Today, you might look at your past and see the darkness. In the future, you will look backward and see a beautiful life with God. This transformation was my story. After several decades of progressive sanctification, God gave me a different identity situated in Christ, not in Adam. What happened to me was real and powerful, but it is not who I am. I am a Christian—a Christ-follower. My past serves redemptive purposes today. Read this list in the CTA—examine your life and walk with Christ. Take the time to reflect and discuss with a friend what you should do to change your past by changing who you are today. Just a few changes can give you a God-honoring future.

Call to Action

1. My past was a path to Jesus.
2. My past is a blessing from the Lord.
3. My past helps me to relate to strugglers.
4. My past motivates me to keep changing.
5. My past encourages me to help others change.
6. My past allows me to warn those who won't change.
7. My past makes me appreciate the grace of God.
8. My past gives me a greater hatred for sin.
9. My past stirs me to long for heaven.
10. My past fills me with the life-altering hope of the gospel.

9

Without Thinking

Doing things without thinking about what we're doing is one of God's greatest favors to us. It is a communicable attribute. God has given us the ability to respond as sentient creatures to the mundane things of life so we can spend our time thinking about the vital things of life. Great habits—developed over time—free us to image God more effectively because they enable us to focus on what is essential for spreading His fame.

Scary Habits

Let's say that you have just arrived at work. Before you get out of the car, you reflect on your commute. You don't remember it. The daily drive is a habit. You've made that trip so many times that your mind releases you from paying attention to the commute. I'm talking about kinesthetic memory. It's the ability to do something without complete cognitive awareness. Some people call it muscle memory. I call it habits. Regardless of how you label it, the Lord gave us this means of grace to help us function at maximum capacity. There are many examples of good habituations.

- You ride a bicycle without looking at the pedals. If your foot slips off, you automatically, without looking, put it back on the pedal.
- You type while looking at the computer screen,

paying no attention to where your fingers land on the keypad.

- You get out of bed each day, giving no thought to going from lying down to walking upright.

It would blow our minds to think about the number of things we do each minute of the day that require no literal thoughts. The Lord did an amazing job creating us. Think again about your drive to work.

- You drive while staying alert to the other drivers.
- You listen to my podcast while pressing the brake pedal.
- You daydream while watching for the light to change and listening to my podcast.
- You observe a dancing lady with a big sign in front of the pawn shop while feeling your phone vibrate because another podcast from our ministry has dropped.
- You review our list of podcasts to ensure you don't miss anything; you also want to share a nugget with your spouse.

I praise you, for I am fearfully and wonderfully made. Wonderful are your works; my soul knows it very well.
(Psalm 139:14)

The upside to habits is that you can't live without them. There is too much going on to be a single-tasking human. Nobody knows this better than a mom with young children. She is not allowed to do one thing at a time. If she could not develop good habits, she would go crazy, literally. Carrying a newborn in her arms and making hot tea while talking to her three-year-old is an art. Oh, and the phone is blasting a tune from her husband, "Another one bites the dust." She responds instinctively, without thinking.

The Downside

Then there is sin, humanity's common adversary. The nature of sin implies that habits are not always good for us. Sometimes, habits take us to destructive places in our lives and relationships. The downside to sinful habits is that we must guard our minds by giving reflective thought to the bad things we do without thinking. More than likely, you do those things because of well-developed patterns. Like the drive to work, you can get in a relational scrape with a friend in a nanosecond, not realizing how you got there because you have developed bad habits. Repentance is never complete until you change those habits.

Too often, a person will sin, confess their sin, and ask for forgiveness, but never change the habits that caused the sin (Ephesians 4:22-24). Repentance means we have changed our old way to a new way that looks like Jesus. We must do more than acknowledge what we did wrong. We must do more than ask the offended for forgiveness. If any sin is a pattern in our lives, we must do the work to unpack the things that have dulled our minds and captured our hearts, keeping us ensconced in bad habits. Sinful habit patterns are our call to think about how we came to the place of mentally disengaged bad behavior.

The Overeating Habit

This need to know is why I write about the motivations of the heart that lead us to do the things we do. If we eat too much, weigh too much, or have other sinful practices, we must deal with the underlying patterns of the heart while interacting—secondarily—with the behaviors. So, let's delve more into our behaviors and how our habits give shape to them. If you're going to change, you must dig deep to get at the heart-motivated causes of your habits. I will use the sin of overeating to illustrate, but you can apply these ideas to any bad behavior. Anger, porn, oversleeping, and smoking are four common bad practices that tempt us to indulge ourselves. I want you to substitute whatever your bad habit is with my illustration of overeating.

Mable is overweight. She knows it but does not know what to do about it. Mable read my thoughts on overeating and seems to be getting a handle on her anxiousness and worry patterns—the heart issues that feed her desire to eat too much. She also understands her craving for comfort and control, which are born out of a spirit of fear. However, Mable continues to eat more than she should. She has not addressed those un-perceived thoughts that trigger her to go for food. Mable is like a sleepwalker. She moves about her home, nibbling to scarfing, without realizing what she is doing. Though she may be tacitly aware, she doesn't fully understand it. Her habits are part of her psyche—her soul: the non-organic part of her. Because all habits work this way, she cannot change until she wakes up and realizes what she is doing to herself while in this soul sleep.

Counseling the Habituated

Habits can be what we do every day and can also be what we do seasonally. Our seasonal habituations could be just as detrimental—holidays, birthdays, or anniversaries. For many of our brothers and sisters, the Christmas holiday is the stimulus for bad habits. They eat too much because of the ubiquity of food. For others, it's their first season without someone, so they indulge themselves. These bad habits can become the everyday makeup of a person's life. It is who they are. Perhaps you know someone like this and are not surprised by their actions. Over time, you accept them as they are without helping them overcome their caught-ness (Galatians 6:1-2). There are three primary reasons for not being a better friend:

- You are afaid to address the caught person.
- You don't know how to help the caught person.
- You don't realize the person is in a trap.

If you want to help them, you must look for their trigger points when addressing their habituated patterns (everyday lifestyle habits). Trigger points are what happens to people that motivate them to develop their habits. Here are a few examples:

- **EXAMPLE #1:** A guy trained himself to look at porn every time his wife leaves home. After she leaves, something inside him begins to burn. It is like the world's largest magnet pulling him to his computer screen.
- **EXAMPLE #2:** A lady trained herself to sleep when things get tough. When life circumstances become challenging, she escapes through sleeping. After a decade of avoiding conflict, she is like a drug addict taking a drug-induced trip. She sleeps through life, hoping things will change.
- **EXAMPLE #3:** The angry spouse's wife trained herself to eat in response to her husband's displeasure. She felt unsafe and wanted comfort. Her God-given desire for love was soured, so she turned to sweets. What she meant for good became an evil means of solace.
- **EXAMPLE #4:** A teen lives in a dysfunctional home. His parents always bicker with each other, and he has no way to leave. Video gaming has become his go-to habit. Now, he's addicted; his grades are falling.

All four people wrongly responded to the trigger points in their lives. At one time, they probably could have walked away from their negative responses to sin, but now they can't. They used to be in control, but now their habits control them. Their sinful reactions to sin go unnoticed as the lady who does not remember her morning drive to work. She arrives and reflects on the journey, amazed she made it without killing someone. The overeater finishes the ice cream and reflects on what she did. Her sad soul state motivates her to eat more—another bad habit.

Practical Tips

Brothers, if anyone is caught in any transgression, you who are spiritual should restore him in a spirit of gentleness. Keep watch on yourself, lest you too be tempted. Bear one another's burdens, and so fulfill the law of Christ. For if anyone thinks he is something, when he is nothing, he deceives himself.
(Galatians 6:1-3)

The first thing to do for the habituated person is to talk with them about their habituation. Draw attention to what is going on in their lives. Help them see the benefits and liabilities of habits. They must understand how the Lord gave them habits to survive and how the devil twisted the Lord's kindness to destroy them (John 10:10). As they gain clarity, they begin unpacking the process that habituated them. Start with the trigger points—the things they do when temptation comes. Discover the sinful stimuli motivating them to respond to problems with bad practices. Discern their caught-ness. If this is the beginning stage of bad habits, it won't be hard to stem the tide. However, if this has been a habituation for many years, your work will be challenging. Walk through all the triggers. There may be more than one, especially if they have developed a pattern of wrong responses to adverse circumstances.

Typically, there may be only one trigger in the beginning— the angry husband. In this scenario, the wife began to eat after each time he railed at her. Overeating became her habit. With no one challenging her response to his sin, she began to eat when any conflict, difficulty, or unnerving situation came into her life. Now, she is controlled and managed by many triggers. You want to spend time with her to talk about all the negative situations in her life and how she habitually responds. She is genuinely caught in her sin, though the original cause was not her fault. Make sure this is clear to her. She is the sinning victim—a person who sins in response to being sinned against. She needs to cultivate the awareness to recognize what is happening to her and how she responds to her husband's actions.

This process takes much prayer. She must regularly engage the Spirit, asking Him to illuminate her mind to what is happening in these moments. It would be great if she learned the habits of pre-praying, present praying, and post-praying after the trigger passes. These are cultivated attitudes and behaviors of prayer before the temptation comes, during the temptation, and after it leaves. Whether she fails or not, she must become a prayer warrior to break this habitation. Passive obedience is not enough. She must actively engage God. Teach her other godly habits, too. For the overeater, she can make healthy selections like carrots, apples, oranges, or celery. She does not have to stop eating but must eat more nutritiously. Finally, teach her about the grace of God that works in her failures because she will fail. Encourage her. Let her know it's okay to fail. She is not going for unbroken, idealized perfection; she is going for gradual transformation. She will never be perfect. She wants to create a pattern of positive habits while factoring in the possibility of episodic failures.

Call to Action

When helping the habituated, ensure they agree to allow you to speak into their lives. Changing years of bad habits will take much work, and they cannot do it alone. Make plans to connect with them occasionally. As they progress, you may be able to address the other issues, too, but for now, you need to stabilize them by helping them break the current bad habit.

1. What are the upsides of habits? Name a few of yours.
2. What are the downsides of habits? Name a few of yours.
3. How did you develop good habits, and how did you develop bad habits?
4. What do you need to do to change your bad habits?
5. What is your specific and practical plan to change?

Conclusion

When your heart is not being obedient because you "just don't feel like doing the right thing," you need to be obedient anyway to get your heart in the right place. We've all had those times of being out-of-sorts and apathetic about doing the right thing. It's not a posture of the heart to applaud, but how do you move forward when desires are low? In such cases, rote, black-and-white obedience is a great way to change what's going on inside of you.

A few years ago I was sharing with a friend about how difficult it was to discipline our kids. Because he was a friend, there was a relational bridge for him to speak truth into my life, and he did. My friend was kind and caring but clear and direct. He said,

> Rick, as a dad, I understand how difficult it can be to discipline children, but your resistance to discipline reveals more about your theology than anything else.

As I considered his well-placed words, I came to four conclusions about how true biblical theology conflicted with my understanding and practice of theology.

- I must fulfill obedience requirements regardless of how I feel about them.

- My understanding of biblical love was not complete. There is a toughness to loving someone well. According to Isaiah 53:10, it pleased the Father to crush His Son.
- My weak theological foundation about love weakened my parenting.
- My understanding of the theology of suffering needed to mature (Genesis 50:20).

The Lord knew that a cross for Christ was a hard and difficult experience (Hebrews 2:14-15). He also knew it was necessary because it was the way to salvation. Sometimes theology is hard, painful, and even emotionally difficult to fulfill (Luke 22:42). But that should not be an excuse for us to shrink back from practicing sound theology. Regarding my particular parenting case, it would be unloving not to step up and discipline our children lovingly when they need corrective care. Are there times in your life when your feelings about a matter cancel out your biblical obedience?

Let me give you another example: I do not enjoy hearing myself speak. I have said that I would not walk across the street to listen to me teach. Perhaps you've heard yourself on a recording and had similar thoughts. In those moments of angst about hearing myself, I could choose never to step on a stage and teach again, a response that would be unwise and counter to the Christian commission to go into all the world and make disciples (Matthew 28:16-20). If I opted for self-centeredness, I would disobey God by not telling others about the glories of Calvary.

Call to Action

Is there an area where you need to be obedient about a matter even though your emotions are lagging behind? Name one of those things. Here are a few examples for your consideration:

1. Confessing your sin to another person when you don't feel motivated to do so?
2. Forgiving someone who has sinned against you when you feel you are right and he is dead wrong?
3. Caving to people-pleasing rather than taking a stand for God because you know taking a stand for what you believe will have repercussions?
4. Refusing to tell someone about the "foolish" Christ (1 Corinthians 1:18) because you're afraid of how they may respond to you?

Being feeling-driven means our thinking is not in line with the gospel. There are times when we permit those sinful thoughts to drive how we respond to God and others. We might use language like "I don't feel like it." If this is a temptation for you, there are two things to consider:

1. Your feelings reveal your thinking. Thus, you must repent of sinful thinking, which will alter your emotions.
2. One way to jumpstart the process is to do what you know to do, anticipating your feelings will eventually change because you chose to be obedient regardless of how you feel about the matter.

When our thoughts are not in line with God's Word, obedience may not come easily. But obedience that flows from faith is still obedience—even when it begins without strong desire. There will be seasons when your heart lags behind, reluctant and slow to move. In those moments, you don't wait for your emotions to catch up—you lead your heart by submitting your mind to the truth and walking it out. Transformation often begins with obedience that seems small, quiet, and even mechanical. But in time, that obedience becomes the pathway to renewed thinking, restored joy, and deepened faith.

This book was written to help you engage in that process—to give you practical tools for identifying, rejecting, and replacing thoughts that oppose the knowledge of God. I trust these pages have served you well in that aim. But this work is ongoing. Our minds remain active, and the spiritual war for our thoughts is relentless. I encourage you to return to these principles often, using this resource as a training ground for continued maturity in Christ. Better yet, teach what you've learned to someone else. Invite a friend into the journey. Help them bring their thoughts into obedience to Christ, just as you are learning to do. This conjoined effort is how we grow together—as disciples who think rightly, love sacrificially, and walk faithfully in step with our Savior.

About the Author

Rick Thomas launched the Life Over Coffee global training network in 2008 to bring hope and help for you and others by creating resources that spark conversations for transformation. His primary responsibilities are resource creation and leadership development, which he does through speaking, writing, podcasting, and educating. In 1990 he earned a BA in Theology and, in 1991, a BS in Education. In 1993, he received his ordination into Christian ministry, and in 2000, he graduated with an MA in Counseling from The Master's University. In 2006, he was recognized as a Fellow of the Association of Certified Biblical Counselors (ACBC).

Other Books Available from
Life Over Coffee

Boasting in Weakness
Centering Your Marriage on Christ
Communication
Complete Marriage
Don't Apologize
Exchange the Truth for a Lie
Help My Marriage Has Grown Cold
Identity Crisis
Local Church
Loving Me
Mad
Marriage Devotion We Are One
Politics and Culture
Parenting Devotion from Zero to Adulthood
Sex, Temptation, and Modesty
Storm Hurler
The Cyber Effect
The Talk
Wives Leading
You Decide